CHART SENSE

Common Sense Charts to Teach Informational Text and Literature

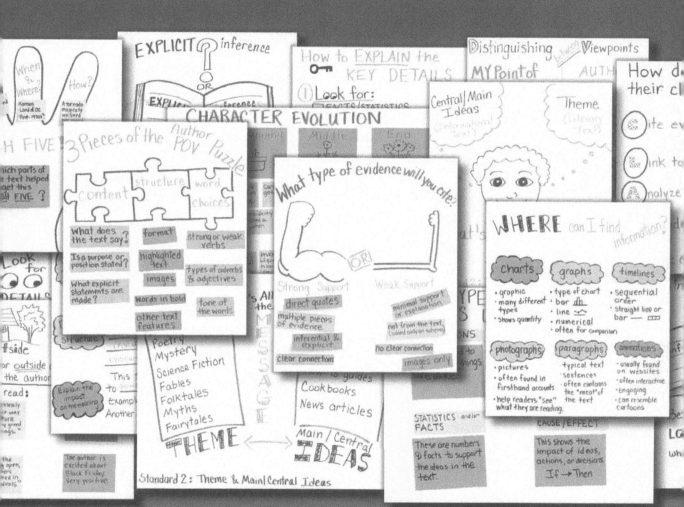

Over 65 Chart Photographs with Scaffolding Tips and Teaching Strategies

Rozlyn Linder

CHART SENSE

Common Sense Charts to Teach 3-8 Informational Text and Literature

Rozlyn Linder, Ph.D.

The Literacy Initiative

Atlanta

Chart Sense: Common Sense Charts to Teach 3-8 Informational Text and Literature
www.ChartSense.RozLinder.com

CHART SENSE is a trademark of The Literacy Initiative, LLC.
541 Tenth Street Suite 258, Atlanta, Georgia 30318

Cover and Interior Design: Buzz Branding, LLC.

Library of Congress Cataloging-in-Publication Data
CIP data is on file with the Library of Congress.
ISBN: 978-0-9889505-1-1

Printed in the U. S. A.

For my husband Chris,
who always sees the very best in me.

Introduction: A Note from Roz

This book is designed as a resource to help you create effective charts that support the informational text and literature standards. The first section, *Why Charts?* explains why charts make a difference in the 3-8 reading classroom. There is also a detailed list and explanation of the materials that you need to create and display effective charts.

Each subsequent chapter is devoted to a different reading standard. The chapters are labeled to match the exact standard that it represents. For example, chapter one is all about reading standard one; chapter two is all about reading standard two; and so on. This allows you to easily turn directly to the standard that you need.

Once you turn to the chapter that you need, the very first page of the chapter lists the Common Core anchor standard. Anchor standards are the broad, overarching standards that apply to all grade levels. Underneath the anchor standard are the literature and informational text standards broken down by grade level. You can easily find your grade level, highlight your standard, and review the specific language of that standard. The standards are worded exactly as they are on the Common Core State Standards Initiative website, sponsored by the National Governors Association Center for Best Practices (NGA Center) and the Council of Chief State School Officers (CCSSO). You can access this directly at: http://www.corestandards.org.

Each additional page features a different instructional chart specific to the reading standard. Detailed notes are provided to explain how the chart can help readers, how to create your own chart, and any grade-level specifications for that chart.

While there are many different charts included here, the idea is not for you to create each chart! The goal is to give you some ideas to support instruction. These charts can be duplicated exactly as they are pictured here or varied and adapted for your classroom. If you adapt a chart or create an even more dynamic version, reach out to let me know! I am always excited to see and hear what new ideas and creative instructional decisions teachers make. Questions? Need help? Reach out to me online at www.rozlinder.com. Happy teaching!

Dr. Roz

Why Charts?

There are so many benefits to using charts in upper elementary and middle school classrooms! With the new, challenging Common Core reading standards, students need more support than ever to make sense of complex text. Shared visuals are an easy and effective way to help support readers. I find that students have a stronger sense of ownership over the content, use the charts as learning tools more often, and are more engaged and interested.

1. Students will have a shared sense of ownership over the content.

You are creating these charts *with* your students. This is not a situation where you tell them to do something and hope that they do it. This is something that you create with your students through discussion, questioning, and a shared sense of learning. You will notice that students revel in having their writing on a chart or recognizing the sections that they contributed to. When a shared chart falls off the wall, your students will actually rush to pick it up and get it back into place. These shared creations will belong to the entire class.

2. Students will use the charts!

You can easily visit your favorite school supply store to stock up on lots of charts to decorate the walls of your classroom. Those charts may be attractive, but do they really impact instruction? How many times have you seen a student use one of those commercial charts? Five? Ten? Make one chart *with* your students, and watch how many more times they use that chart!

3. Visuals are engaging!

Charts give students a visual reminder of what is expected, how to get there, and ways to troubleshoot. Often, students may not ask for help or admit that they don't remember a strategy. Having a consistent visual reminder is an appealing way to trigger their memories and to keep their attention. Think about the typical fashion magazine. Some of these magazines are 50% advertisements! From a financial standpoint that infuriates me, but I still catch myself gazing at the attractive spreads to see what they are selling. My curiosity is piqued, and I actually keep the image in my head. Creating an attractive visual *with* your students is just one way to tap into that same phenomenon, but for reading.

Different Types of Charts

There are many different types of charts. They can be organized and classified in a dozen (or more) different ways by a dozen (or more) different experts. For grades 3-8, I like to think about charts as reminders for students. They help students to keep track of their learning and to apply it. Relying on this belief, I classify charts into four key areas:

1. **Ritual**

2. **Toolbox**

3. **Classification**

4. **Interactive**

Ritual

These types of traditional charts can be found in virtually every K-12 classroom. Ritual charts usually display the basic rules that students should follow. These can include behavior, classroom expectations, or arrival/dismissal procedures. Many of the procedural charts that teachers make for writing and reading workshops often fall into this category as well. Ritual charts are introduced at the beginning of the year or unit, and they rarely change. These charts, while important, are very specific to your own classroom. They will vary based on the norms, beliefs, and programs adopted by your school and district. As a result, *Chart Sense* does not include this type of chart.

Toolbox

Toolbox charts remind me of a day, not too long ago, when I watched a car mechanic pulling out his red, weathered toolbox to try to diagnose my car. The tattered toolbox seemed to be filled with everything he needed. I watched with curiosity as he lifted my hood, then proceeded to pull out a wide variety of tools. I found myself questioning and wondering what exactly was going on. What was that black thing? Why does he have two of those? What is that pointy thing? Why did he put that tool back in the box?

Toolbox chart example

Readers also rely on a toolbox of strategies and steps that help them make meaning of text. Toolbox charts represent that collection of strategies. Readers certainly aren't fixing a car with these tools, but they are just as powerful. Toolbox charts help students to understand options for what to do when they struggle, get confused, or need help determining what to do next. These types of charts could include steps to follow when working on a specific standard or problem-solving strategies. Toolbox charts are introduced throughout the year. They can help you introduce a unit of study or serve as activators. These charts are also created in response to student performance. If I notice that most of my readers are coming to a roadblock when they encounter new vocabulary, I may develop a chart that helps them understand the concrete steps that they need to follow when they encounter a new word. I often add additional information to these charts throughout the year as students develop new reading skills and tools.

Classification

Classification charts can be used when your students need to understand unique or different characteristics. For example, genre charts that list the features of fantasy or mystery books would fit in this category. Classification charts are also useful when students need to compare and contrast. Teachers can use these to help students keep track of big ideas and distinguish concepts. Students use these charts as visuals that show how two ideas or concepts are different. These can be in the form of lists, Venn diagrams, or other graphics. Classification charts can also be used to develop initial understanding or to redirect a misunderstanding. They can be introduced at any time throughout the year.

Classification chart example

Interactive

Interactive charts are my absolute favorite. I find that students learn the most from these types of charts. Interactive charts can be static or reusable. Students generate the information, and it is specific to a particular text. For example, if I teach my students to craft summaries about a book, we would also create a chart to go along with it. This chart would be a summary (or portion of a summary) that we would write as a class. This collaborative process results in meaningful charts that differ from year to year. Not only are these charts created *with the students,* but they also include an active think-aloud modeling session. Think-aloud modeling means that as you write, you stop to question, wonder, and let students have a peek into your cognitive process. Interactive charts usually remain in a prominent place, and they serve as exemplars.

Interactive chart example

Sticky notes work hand-in-hand with this type of chart. For example, as students read books and talk about their reading, they can use sticky notes to record their ideas and thoughts. Interactive charts are great spaces to share and post these ideas. The sticky notes can also be removed or repositioned depending on the book or new standard that your class is focusing on.

Please keep in mind that each of these different chart categories are not rigid boxes that must remain separate. There will be overlap, and some charts could belong in more than one category. The category is not the most important thing here; the teaching is.

Materials to Create Great Charts

It is not necessary to be an artist or to spend tons of money to create effective charts for your readers. There are some basic tools that you will want to have on hand to make charts easily.

Chart Paper

This is a given! Let's talk about the different styles. There are brands that have adhesive on the back and can be stuck right onto the wall. These work well, but they will eventually lose their adhesive quality and possibly fall down. This process will happen even faster if you move your charts around a lot. The easy solution is to add tape. *But…if I have to add tape, then I might as well use regular chart paper, right?* Well, there are pros and cons to all types of chart paper. Let's take a look:

Paper Type	Benefits	Disadvantages
Adhesive-Back Chart Paper	You can quickly attach these to any wall in seconds. These are readily available in most office supply stores.	These may eventually fall down without the addition of more tape. This is the most expensive choice.
Non-Adhesive Chart Paper	Most school and office supply stores carry this paper. This is the most inexpensive choice.	You must use tape or magnets to display this type of chart.
Half-Sized Chart Paper	These are great for quick charts that don't require a full-size sheet.	You may still need to purchase full-size paper for larger charts.
Non-Adhesive Colored Chart Paper	These bright charts are the most attractive of all the options.	A limited number of stores carry this paper. This is more expensive than plain white chart paper.

Sticky Notes

Sticky notes are essential when creating reusable charts. They can easily be filled out in advance and repositioned as necessary. In order to maximize this flexibility, I try to keep a wide variety on hand. Post-it® brand notes are readily available in many shapes, sizes, and colors. One of my favorites is the large 8"x6" size. This size does cost more, but it really helps your charts stand out and offers a lot of space to write on. A cheaper alternative to emulate the effect of this oversized sticky note is to grab a pack of colored paper and tape. You can cut the paper into any shape or size, then use a small amount of tape to stick the note onto your chart. Another cost-cutting alternative is to buy the store-brand sticky notes at a discount or dollar store.

Thin-Tip Markers

I like to have thin, student-friendly markers on hand. These markers work best for your students to use when they need to write on the charts or add information. These thin markers also come in handy when you need to illustrate something more elaborate or draw a simple detail. Crayola®, Rose Art®, and Sharpie® all sell great thin-tip markers. I have even found several office supply store brands to work just as well.

Wide-Tip Markers

I use wide-tip markers most frequently when writing on charts. I have tried many different brands, shapes, and sizes. This choice really comes down to personal preference. For a long time, I relied only on the scented Mr. Sketch® markers. In the past few years I have also discovered the wide-tip Sharpie® brand markers. Both brands are excellent choices for making charts. Be careful to avoid any markers that are labeled as "poster markers." These tend to be much too big for charts, and they also bleed through chart paper.

Sentence Strips

Sentence strips are long pieces of sturdy paper, resembling cardstock. One side has a guideline rule, while the other has a single line. You can find sentence strips in white, beige, rainbow, and pastel colors at school supply stores and big-box retailers. They only cost a few dollars and one pack goes a long way.

In the nineties, when I first started creating charts with my students, I never even thought about adding sentence strips to a chart. Why would I do that? Couldn't I just write the same information on the actual chart or on a sticky note? Eventually, I found that sentence strips were surprisingly useful when making charts. They are larger than most sticky notes and much more durable. They also come in handy when students need to record more than just a few words on a chart. There are times when you will need to add book titles, long phrases, or even lengthy passages of text to a chart. Sentence strips provide the extra space necessary to do this.

Scissors

You want to keep a pair of reliable scissors on hand. There will be times when you will need to use them to cut your sticky notes and sentence strips into various shapes and sizes. Make sure that you have a few extra pairs for student use as well.

Adhesive

Masking tape is a useful resource to keep on hand. You will need this to hold charts up and attach paper to the charts. I prefer this type of tape because it can easily be removed when you need to reposition different elements of your chart. If you are a fan of clear or double-sided tape, be certain that what you are taping down does not need to be manipulated by your students often. The last thing you want to do is rip a hole in one of your charts.

Space for Charts

Every classroom is arranged differently, and school districts have varied rules about how wall space can be used. Optimally, you will have lots of blank walls and the ability to put as much (or as little) on the walls as you choose. In reality, this is rarely the case. It is usually necessary to explore alternative options for displaying your charts. If your students cannot see the charts, they can't use them. Here are some of the ways I display my charts.

The Clothesline

I first started using the clothesline method when I was a fourth-grade teacher. I bought an actual clothesline at a big-box retailer, two nails, and plastic clothespins. I asked our wonderful custodian if he would place the two nails in opposite corners of my room. We hung a clothesline that spanned the length of my classroom. I learned a few valuable lessons that year. When you hang such a long clothesline diagonally, only half of the class can see any particular chart at the same time. I also learned that chart paper doesn't like to stay attached to a clothesline without reinforcement. One chart actually took four or five plastic clothespins to stay in place. Also, this meant that our entire class was always drowning under a sea of charts.

The next year I reworked my whole clothesline idea. I had to admit that I'd grown overly attached to my charts, and just wanted my handiwork visible at all times! That was the wrong approach; I had to let it go. This time I hung the clothesline flat against one wall. I learned that I did not need every chart hanging up at the same time. Only charts that students are actively using need to be displayed in a classroom.

Magnets

One simple way to display your charts is to hang them on a chalkboard or a whiteboard using magnets. Two or three magnets will easily hold up most charts. The use of magnets gives you the flexibility to post and remove your charts as needed. This also allows metal file cabinets or any other metal surfaces in your classroom to become display areas.

Hangers

Skirt or pants hangers work well to display charts. You should be able to inexpensively pick up a few at the local dollar store. When buying clothing from any retailer, ask the cashier if you can keep your hangers. You can even ask for some of the extra hangers that are almost always in a big box under the cash register. I have walked out of stores with over thirty pants hangers. It doesn't hurt to ask!

Once you have your hangers, you can use them to easily hang any non-laminated charts. Laminated charts tend to be slippery and will slide out of the clips. You can store your charts by hanging them out of the way on doors or cabinets until you need them. You can also use a garment stand to hold the hangers. I like this idea because your students can go over and access any chart that they need, even after you retire it from the wall. If you live close to an IKEA, consider purchasing a *Rigga* or a *Mulig* clothing stand. Both stands cost around ten dollars apiece and can even be ordered online at www.ikea.com.

Hidden Gems

Don't overlook the obvious. A chart can be displayed in many different places. If you have fabric curtains covering a bookcase, grab two safety pins and attach your chart to the front of the curtain. Depending on how your room is organized, the marker or chalk holder at the base of your chalkboard or whiteboard is a perfect space to hang several charts. Do you have large classroom cabinets? The doors and sides of those cabinets could be great landing spots for charts. Check out your classroom windows, the front of your desk, the bottom of a mounted television, or even the extra space above your chalkboard. Think about places that normally go untouched. Be creative and look for hidden gems!

Chapter 1

Textual Evidence

Common Core Reading Anchor Standard 1:
Read closely to determine what the text says explicitly and make logical inferences from it; cite specific textual evidence when writing or speaking to support conclusions drawn from the text.

	Literary Text	Informational Text
3rd	Ask and answer questions to demonstrate understanding of a text, referring explicitly to the text as the basis for the answers.	Ask and answer questions to demonstrate understanding of a text, referring explicitly to the text as the basis for the answers.
4th	Refer to details and examples in a text when explaining what the text says explicitly and when drawing inferences from the text.	Refer to details and examples in a text when explaining what the text says explicitly and when drawing inferences from the text.
5th	Quote accurately from a text when explaining what the text says explicitly and when drawing inferences from the text.	Quote accurately from a text when explaining what the text says explicitly and when drawing inferences from the text.
6th	Cite textual evidence to support analysis of what the text says explicitly as well as inferences drawn from the text.	Cite textual evidence to support analysis of what the text says explicitly as well as inferences drawn from the text.
7th	Cite several pieces of textual evidence to support analysis of what the text says explicitly as well as inferences drawn from the text.	Cite several pieces of textual evidence to support analysis of what the text says explicitly as well as inferences drawn from the text.
8th	Cite the textual evidence that most strongly supports an analysis of what the text says explicitly as well as inferences drawn from the text.	Cite the textual evidence that most strongly supports an analysis of what the text says explicitly as well as inferences drawn from the text.

Explicit or Inference?

This is such a great visual for all grade levels to use. When students have book talks and really dig into a text, I like to eavesdrop on their conversations, interjecting to ask if the information they share and discuss is explicit or inferred. Students immediately look at this chart, and I can almost see them mentally checking off the characteristics of each. This really takes something that feels abstract and makes it much more tangible and easy to quantify.

Introducing This Chart:

1. Before I write anything on the chart, I have a conversation with my students. My conversation usually begins like this: *"I want everyone to be completely silent and watch me. I am going to walk around and I want you to think about what types of decisions you can make about me based on clues (evidence) that you notice. We are going to call those decisions inferences."*

2. I spend 2-3 minutes demonstrating a strong dislike or like for something in the room. I typically select one gender or one side of the room that I demonstrate a preference for. As I circulate around the room, I offer visual clues to indicate which group I prefer. I ham it up and have some fun here. If it doesn't feel silly, you aren't doing it right! This activity should be light-hearted and fun.

3. When we are done, students will identify that I had a preference for one side of the room over the other. I challenge them, almost defiantly, about this inference. *"How do you know? I didn't say that! What evidence do you have?"*

4. As students share responses, I point out that my preference for one side was an inference. I explain that inferences are not directly stated; you have to look for clues. This is when we create the chart together, and discuss each characteristic.

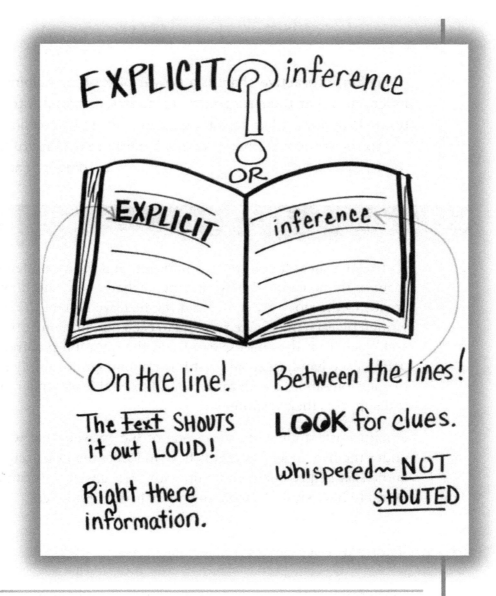

Figure 1.1 *Explicit or Inference?* chart

High Five!

This fun, interactive chart is a powerful tool for helping students understand that their responses to questions about a text require textual support. I like to introduce this chart by reading out loud to my students. I begin with a familiar text that students have studied or can relate to.

Introducing This Chart:

As I read a short literature selection out loud to my students, I ask them to think about who, what, when, where, why, and how in reference to the story. After we read the text, we look at the question written on each finger. We respond to each question on a sticky note and place it on the chart. Next, I add the question pictured in the palm of the hand. I explain that it is not enough to simply respond to questions about a text; readers need to be able to explain how the text supports their responses.

Finally, I ask students to select one of the answers that we posted under the five fingers. Students have to locate the exact sentence or quote that helped them come up with their answers. It can also be useful to have students write down the textual evidence.

Extension Activities:

1. Determine if the answers on each finger are inferences or if the information was explicit in the text.

2. Draw a hand and photocopy it to add to a literacy center. Students can complete this when they read independently.

3. A blank version of this chart can be laminated and reused for multiple texts.

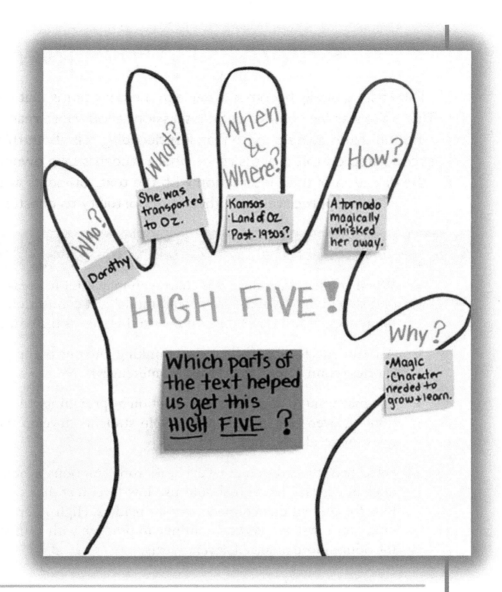

Figure 1.2 *High Five!* chart

Stepping Up the Evidence!

This chart typically becomes a staple in the classrooms that I work with. This is the starting point to begin discussions about close reading and the notion that reading is more than just decoding; it is about thinking. The second step on this chart is really where students take ownership over the direction of their interaction with the text. Students also begin to appreciate the authentic opportunity to question the text.

Teaching Tips:

- When you first introduce this chart, you may want to break the second step up into chunks. You could model just connections, or just inferences, or just questions. Add on to this step as the year goes on.

- Ask students to classify their own thinking into one of the three categories (connections, questions, or inferences).

- You may want to differentiate instruction by providing guiding questions or even sentence frames to help students develop their own questions and inferences.

- Select texts to read aloud that evoke a strong emotional reaction. This does not mean that you should use low-level text, but you should look for content that connects to your readers. High-interest is *not* a proxy for low-level. As you continue to practice with your students, introduce more nuanced, layered texts.

Grade Level Considerations:

This chart works well for each grade level. I have used a version of this chart with high school students to lead them in a modified version of text annotation. For third graders, the standard focuses on asking and answering questions for step two. They do not need to explicitly make inferences or connections.

Figure 1.3 *Stepping Up the Evidence!* chart

Textual Evidence Sentence Starters

This simple chart is my most popular chart. Whenever I do workshops, teachers rush to photograph it. After one particular workshop, I went to visit the classrooms of several teachers who were planning to use this chart with their fifth graders. When I arrived, they were overjoyed to share their charts. To my surprise, it was my exact chart, blown up and laminated in each classroom. They were so very proud. I hated to be the bearer of bad news, but they had missed the whole point. This is not a cute chart to hang in the classroom! The whole point is to create the chart *with* your students.

Using This Chart:

When I create this chart in the classroom, we add one starter at a time and discuss it. Next, we revisit fairy tales or picture books that we have read, taking turns completing the sentence starters about those familiar texts. This rich interaction builds a sense of shared ownership over the chart and makes each sentence starter resonate more with students.

Grade Level Considerations:

This chart is effective for any grade level. I find that seventh and eighth graders are often not given sentence starters. The general idea is that they are beyond that, but this could not be further from the truth. The sentence starters offer support and a concrete way to scaffold your instruction.

Teaching Tip:

This is a chart to keep visible in your classroom all year long. This becomes a staple that really does get used often! In fact, students will be expected to provide textual evidence when they work with almost every reading standard.

Figure 1.4 *Textual Evidence Sentence Starters*

Thinking About Text!

This simple chart is great for all grade levels. The language of the standard asks that students use the words from the text to support their thinking. I like to read a short informational or literary text out loud to my students. The text we read for this chart was Seymour Simon's *Volcanoes*.

Selecting a Text:

Make sure that students have their own copies of the text as well. This is a great time to turn to your science or social studies text when introducing this part of the lesson. If you have a book that you don't have multiple copies of, use a document camera or photocopy a few pages so that students can have the same text in front of them.

Teaching This Concept:

1. Explain that when people make decisions based on evidence, this is called an **inference.** *"As we read, I want you to make some decisions, or inferences, about this text."*

2. After you read the text, call on students to share inferences along with the textual evidence to support that inference.

3. As they share, write their inferences on large sticky notes and add them to the chart.

Teaching Tips:

- This chart is interactive and can be used over and over again if you only record information on the sticky notes.

- Repeat frequently with different parts of the book or other books as needed.

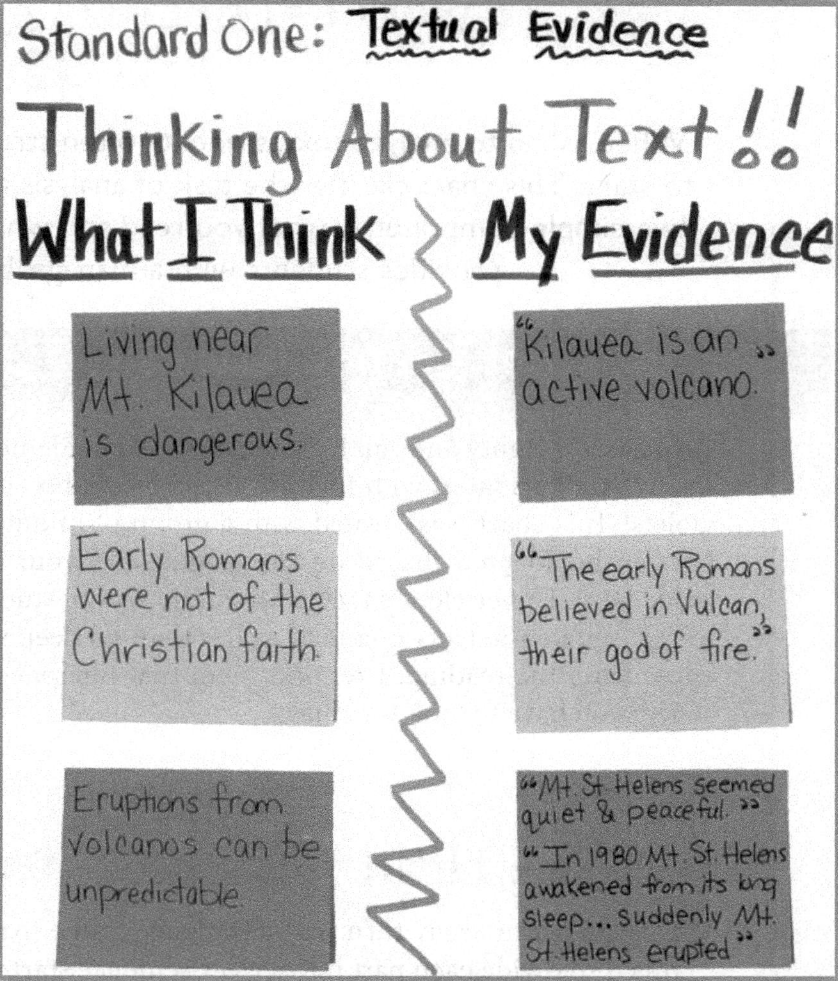

Figure 1.5 *Thinking About Text!* chart

The chart reads:

Standard One: Textual Evidence

Thinking About Text!!

What I Think | My Evidence

Living near Mt. Kilauea is dangerous. | "Kilauea is an active volcano."

Early Romans were not of the Christian faith. | "The early Romans believed in Vulcan, their god of fire."

Eruptions from volcanos can be unpredictable. | "Mt. St. Helens seemed quiet & peaceful." "In 1980 Mt. St. Helens awakened from its long sleep... suddenly Mt. St Helens erupted"

What Does it Mean to Analyze Text?

When asked to analyze text, students often struggle with where to start. This chart clarifies the task of analysis and reduces it to two simple components: what you read and what you infer. This provides students with a manageable starting point.

Grade Level Considerations:

Analysis is weighty and can be somewhat scary. Elementary and middle school students faced with the task of analyzing text tend to shrink like violets! This chart was created with a group of middle school students, but can be adapted (based on the language of your standard) for any grade level. Upper elementary and middle school students tend to want to regurgitate the facts in a text, rather than go deeper and make inferences from the reading. I remind them that inferences are not directly stated; you have to look for clues.

Scaffolding Ideas:

1. This chart can easily turn into a sentence frame. An quick way to do this is to divide each part into a clear sentence starter. For example:

    The text says: _____. My inference about this is _____.

    This simple paired sentence frame offers support and a more gradual entry point for your reluctant or struggling readers.

2. One teacher I worked with had students create their own tiny light bulbs and textbook pages to put on their desks to remind them to pair their inference with specific support from the text.

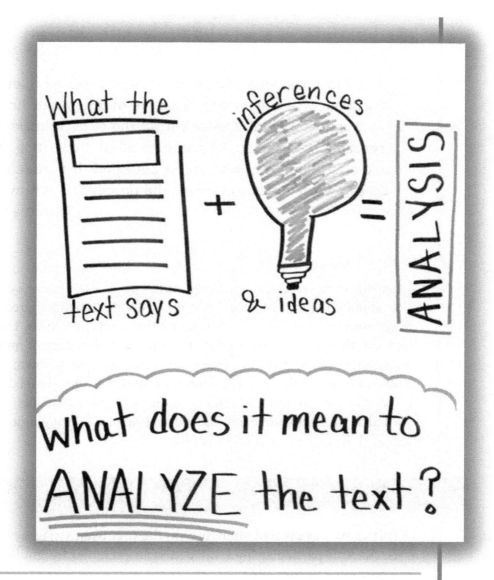

Figure 1.6 *What Does it Mean to Analyze Text?* chart

What I Know

I love the idea of a great visual, like this silhouette, to help students remember that what we decide in our heads can be supported with evidence from the text. To make this chart reusable, we used sticky notes for all of the writing. This chart could also be directly written on, but I find that students need to do this a few times to cement the process, so removable sticky notes work best.

Using This Chart:

After spending several days reading a grade-level text, we had a class discussion about what we now knew and understood. Students shared many different inferences and conclusions about the events and ideas. I wrote these different things down on large sticky notes and placed them on the board. As a group, we selected three inferences. I trimmed them down, so that they would fit inside of the "head" to show our thinking. Then, I asked students to go back to the text and find evidence to support the statements. Afterwards, we had a rich discussion about the textual evidence. Throughout the year, we repeated the activity with other books.

Selecting a Text:

1. This chart was created after reading the first twenty pages of Jon Katz's *Geeks*. This particular book is listed as an exemplar for grades 6-8 in the Common Core appendices.

2. I suggest modeling this with a book that students have had ample time to explore and make sense of.

3. This is a great chart to use when working with graphic novels, any strong archetypal stories, fables, social studies content, or literature with layered characters.

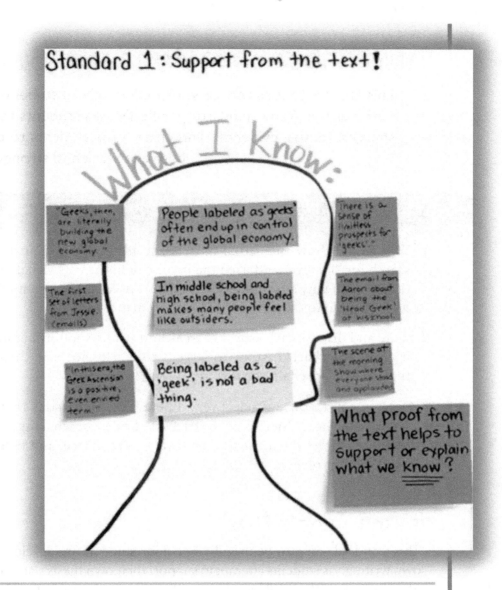

Figure 1.7 *What I Know* chart

What Type of Evidence Will You Cite?

This chart is best suited for your middle school students. In fact, the eighth grade standard specifically asks students to cite the *strongest* textual evidence. This chart helps students to delineate between weak and strong support.

Creating This Chart:

1. You should draw the actual muscles in advance. I did an Internet search for "Popeye" and used the images of his arm as visual inspiration to create my strong support muscle. I used images from *Diary of a Wimpy Kid* to create my weak support arm.

2. Share and discuss each aspect of weak and strong support before adding it to the chart. I wrote on large 8"x6" sticky notes and trimmed them down, based on the text.

3. On your chart, you may select very different characteristics than what I have listed here. There is not a strict set of rules for what fits in either category. Target the areas that you want to reinforce, and tailor this chart to your readers.

Writing Connection:

This standard can also be useful when your students are developing their own writing. As students attempt to support their own thesis statements and ideas as writers, they will have to consider the best way to do this. Referring back to this chart helps them make the connection to reading and writing.

The most obvious connection is to opinion and argument, but evidence is richly interwoven into narratives as well. Consider how characters are crafted in a text. Students can explicitly look at the different types of evidence (details) authors use when they establish a villain or hero. This will help students when they craft their own narratives.

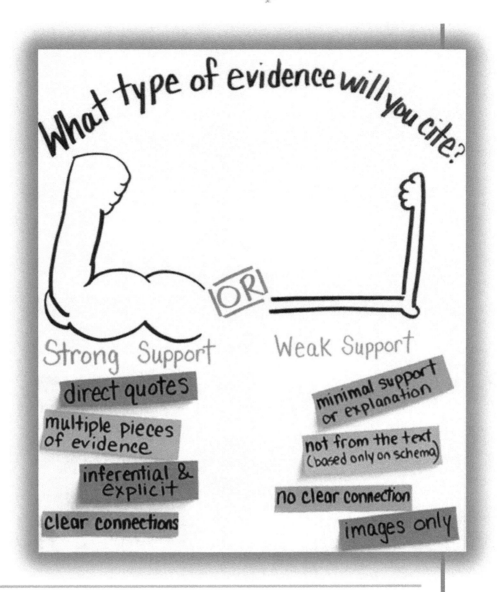

Figure 1.8 *What Type of Evidence Will You Cite?* chart

Chapter 2

Main/Central Idea

Common Core Reading Anchor Standard 2:
Determine central ideas or themes of a text and analyze their development; summarize the key supporting details and ideas.

	Literary Text	Informational Text
3rd	Recount stories, including fables, folktales, and myths from diverse cultures; determine the central message, lesson, or moral and explain how it is conveyed through key details in the text.	Determine the main idea of a text; recount the key details and explain how they support the main idea.
4th	Determine a theme of a story, drama, or poem from details in the text; summarize the text.	Determine the main idea of a text and explain how it is supported by key details; summarize the text.
5th	Determine a theme of a story, drama, or poem from details in the text, including how characters in a story or drama respond to challenges or how the speaker in a poem reflects upon a topic; summarize the text.	Determine two or more main ideas of a text and explain how they are supported by key details; summarize the text.
6th	Determine a theme or central idea of a text and how it is conveyed through particular details; provide a summary of the text distinct from personal opinions or judgments.	Determine a central idea of a text and how it is conveyed through particular details; provide a summary of the text distinct from personal opinions or judgments.
7th	Determine a theme or central idea of a text and analyze its development over the course of the text; provide an objective summary of the text.	Determine two or more central ideas in a text and analyze their development over the course of the text; provide an objective summary of the text.
8th	Determine a theme or central idea of a text and analyze its development over the course of the text, including its relationship to the characters, setting, and plot; provide an objective summary of the text.	Determine a central idea of a text and analyze its development over the course of the text, including its relationship to supporting ideas; provide an objective summary of the text.

How to Explain Key Details

I find that students need concrete patterns to help them make sense of abstract ideas. Looking at key details is one of those tasks that seems very nuanced and abstract for students. This chart is a great tool to help make this task less subjective and easier to think about and explain. I teach students that there is a four-step process to write about the details in an informational text.

Creating This Chart:

I like to make this chart from start to finish with students. I find that collaborative creation is best for the shared sense of ownership over the content and chart. If you have limited time or just don't want to draw the entire chart with the class, go ahead and create the four steps and draw the check boxes. Print the other words in different fonts from your computer and tape them next to the checkboxes as you introduce each one.

Teaching Ideas:

1. Write your own paragraph with the students using a familiar informational text or a short excerpt that you can read in one session. Post this for future reference.

2. This is a great time to sneak in some additional writing instruction by brainstorming ways to craft sentences for step two.

3. Explain that key details do not always just fit into one category or the other. They often overlap and can be classified in many different ways.

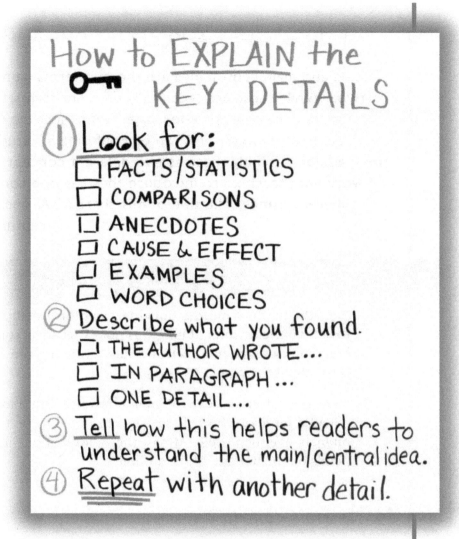

Figure 2.1 *How to Explain Key Details* chart

It's All About the Message

Theme and main/central idea are the two terms named in standard two. While these are technically different terms, both get at the same core concept: **message.** *What does the author want the reader to take away?* This can be confusing for students and even some adults. Teaching these as two different concepts is challenging. I work with teachers to introduce these as one concept with two different names. The title of this chart, *It's All About the Message*, captures this notion.

Teaching Tips:

- Vary the types of informational text and/or literature that you list to suit your classroom. Our list is not exhaustive; some basics, like biographies, have not been included. This list can and will grow throughout the year.

- Note the asterisks next to "memoirs" and "autobiographies." We talked a lot about how these are considered to be true and based on facts. We then explored how the validity of that assumption depends on the honesty of the author.

Main or Central?

For this chart, use the language from your grade-level standard. Main Idea is for elementary students. Central Idea is for middle school students. This chart was created with sixth graders. You will notice that we used both main and central. We chose to do this because these students had just spent the previous year calling this the main idea. Now, as middle school students, the term had shifted to central idea. We wanted them to connect the two ideas and recognize them as synonymous.

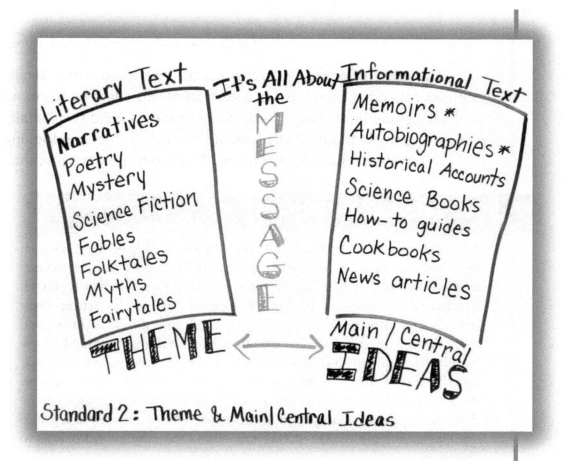

Figure 2.2 *It's All About the Message* chart

Look for Details

This chart offers students a visual to think about what details authors rely on. I have created a version of this chart with almost every grade level. Regardless of age, students need to mentally picture and think about what types of information they are looking for in an informational piece. This fun chart does just that.

Introducing This Chart:

I draw the eyes and the title in advance. I write the types of details with students and explain what each one is. Then, I ask students to read a short article. For this lesson, we read "Five Reasons Not to Drink Bottled Water" by Chris Baskind. I regularly turn to this article when introducing informational text standards because it is straightforward and contains many of the informational text features included in the standards. You can find this article here: http://www.mnn.com/food/healthy-eating/stories/5-reasons-not-to-drink-bottled-water. After we read the text, I put students into groups and ask them to categorize the different types of details found in the article. We reconvene as a group and begin our discussion. As we talk, I add their ideas and details to the chart.

Variations:

1. Give students markers and sticky notes and let them record the details themselves. In order to add them to the class chart, students have to explain why they selected that detail and explain how they categorized it.

2. Instead of a web, turn the chart sideways and make five columns for each category. Add the sticky notes under each column.

3. Create a smaller, blank chart like this one for students to use in pairs or independently when they read their own texts.

Figure 2.3 *Look for Details* chart

Powerful Details

I introduce this to my students as a "secret" method for explaining details. I ask students to elaborate on at least two different details, with an emphasis on describing how those details support the meaning and main/central idea of a text.

Explaining is Hard to Do!

Explaining is a foreign term to many students. What does it mean? Retell? Summarize? Not quite. In order to explain, students need to make some decisions about the text. The tricky part of this standard is that students are indeed asked to summarize the text, but they are also asked to explain the key details. That leaves students with two different tasks: objectively conveying what the text is about and also making decisions about how the details connect, support, and confirm the main/central ideas. This chart is just about the explanation of details. Students can add this to the end of an objective summary, or they can use it as a standalone explanation of the details.

Scaffolding Ideas:

1. I am a big fan of sentence frames. I find that they offer a natural way to gradually release the responsibility of learning. As students assume more responsibility for this task, they can craft their own paragraphs, being certain to include the necessary elements used here.

2. This chart can be turned into a checklist instead of a sentence/paragraph frame.

3. Add additional sentences that require the integration of more textual evidence or even specific types of evidence.

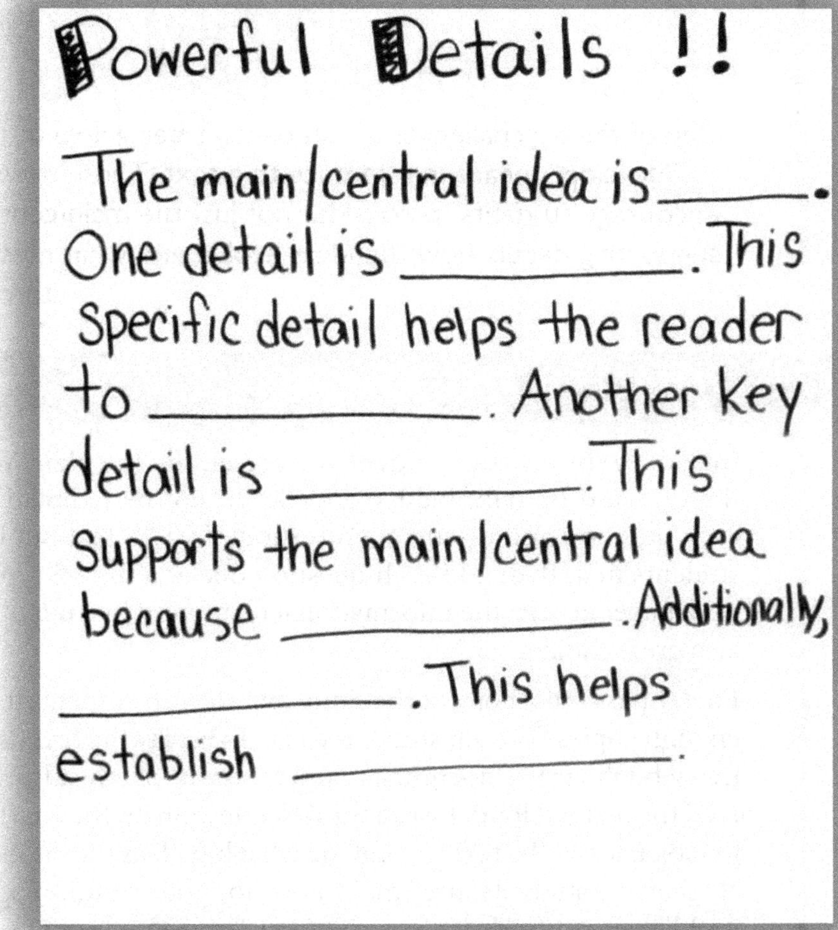

Powerful Details !!

The main/central idea is _____.
One detail is _____. This specific detail helps the reader to _____. Another key detail is _____. This supports the main/central idea because _____. Additionally, _____. This helps establish _____.

Figure 2.4 *Powerful Details* chart

Thinking About How Ideas Develop in a Text

One of the big challenges for students is being able to understand what "develop" means in reference to a text. These five simple questions encourage students to consider not just the main/central ideas, but the supporting details, how the ideas evolve, and what messages are woven throughout the text.

Introducing This Chart:

Introduce this to your students by presenting the blank chart with only the title and thought bubble added. Do not be tempted to simply add each question and discuss it. You should read a text out loud with your students first, then add each question one at a time. I typically choose a newspaper article; the informational text found in student magazines are also great choices.

First, I pass out a copy of the same text to each student. If you don't have enough copies for each student, you can display the text using an interactive whiteboard, a document camera, or an overhead projector. After I read the text out loud, I write the first question on the chart. I ask students to look back in the text and tell me what big ideas they notice. If you teach elementary students, use "main idea" for your terminology. If you teach middle school students, use the term "central idea." After we share our big ideas, we point out the textual evidence that supports those big ideas. Now that we have discussed question one, we can move on to the rest of the questions on the chart.

Free Informational Text Sources:

- **New York Times Education Articles**
  (http://learning.blogs.nytimes.com/)
- **Scholastic News Online**
  (http://teacher.scholastic.com/activities/scholasticnews/index.html)

Figure 2.5 *Thinking About How Ideas Develop in a Text* chart

Thinking About the Main Idea

While terms like "main," "big," or "central" make sense to teachers, these terms remain elusive and vague to many students. This fun chart just asks variations of the same question in different ways. When you use this with your students, you will find that they all will rely on one question that resonates with them. I always find this fascinating. For me, only one question really gets to the heart of a central idea. Invariably, my students rarely connect and "get it" using my question. This speaks volumes about the different ways that we construct meaning and interpret something as simple as a question. What I appreciate most is that students get to choose how they will think about central/main ideas.

Introducing This Chart:

To prepare for this lesson, I only draw the face and thought bubble on the chart. I also like to type up five different paragraphs (about 4-6 sentences long) in advance. I use argumentative topics that my students are very familiar with. When I begin my lesson, I display one paragraph on a projector or whiteboard. After I read the paragraph out loud, I write one of the questions in the thought bubble and we discuss it. This is also a great opportunity to review inferences and textual evidence. I repeat this process, adding a different question to the chart each time.

Variations:

1. Use a group picture or collage of your students in place of the face.

2. Instead of writing five different paragraphs to introduce this chart, select informational text excerpts that present a clear opinion or argument.

3. For the name of this chart, use the terminology from your grade level standard. "Main Idea" is for elementary students. "Central Idea" is for middle school students.

Figure 2.6 *Thinking About the Main Idea* chart

Two Different Ways to Think About Theme

Ask ten different teachers to define theme and you will get ten different answers. There is a logical argument to be made for the multiple definitions and interpretations of theme. I find that different teachers, state assessments, and textbooks present theme very differently. Rather than debate which way is the best, I like to teach students that there are multiple ways to think about theme. This chart classifies theme into two categories. I like to begin by naming the two categories and slowly building the lists over time with my students. As we read new books, I encourage students to identify and describe the theme(s) that they notice.

"Bumper Sticker" Themes:

This type of theme is often found in fables, folktales, myths, and fairy tales. Typically, the moral or lesson is what we often ask students to look for. This category can also be quite subjective. Students are able to draw from their own background knowledge and come up with a wide variety of examples that fit into this category.

Topical Themes:

This category is much broader. I used to teach these as *topics* rather than *themes*. I came to learn that many state assessments, however, often refer to many topics as themes. Any topic can easily be expanded into a complete sentence, making it read much more like a bumper sticker theme. Teach your students to recognize both.

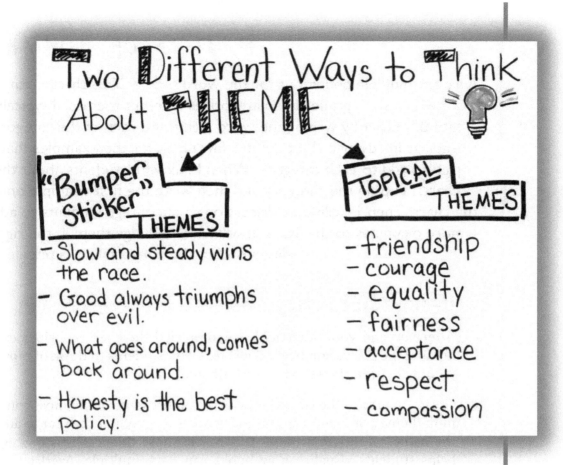

Figure 2.7 *Two Different Ways to Think About Theme* chart

Types of Theme

There are multiple definitions for the word theme. This chart, created with a sixth grade class, categorizes different themes. I typically create this chart by writing the word *theme* and each of the category headings in advance. I jot down a few notes for the examples that I plan to add to each category. When I talk with students about this chart, I explain the category and then write the first example onto the chart. Then, I facilitate a discussion to encourage students to add more examples to the list. You will have to nudge them in the right direction, but the conversation is priceless.

Extension Activities:

- After you and your students have completed the chart, consider extending the discussion beyond just text. Ask students to think of movies or television shows that reflect different themes.

- Create an area in the classroom where you list some of the most common themes. Students can use sticky notes throughout the year to add the names of different books that reflect those themes. This process helps students visualize how books can have multiple, overlapping themes.

Grade Level Considerations:

1. This chart is appropriate for all grade levels.

2. For your third and fourth graders, consider providing less categories.

3. Remember that this is not exhaustive and there are probably a dozen other categories that you could incorporate into this type of chart. Tailor this to your grade level and class.

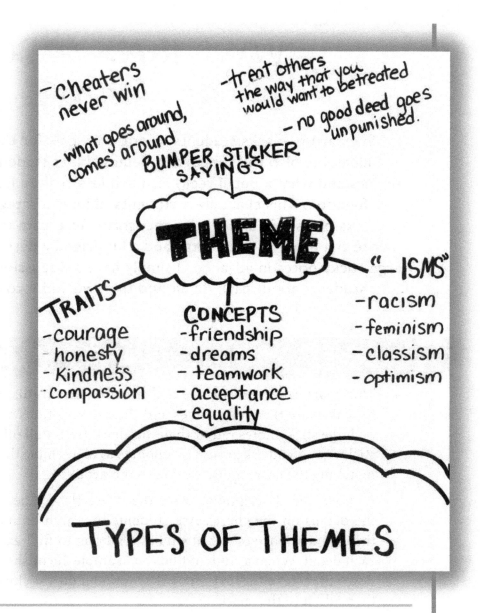

Figure 2.8 *Types of Theme* chart

What Types of Details do Authors Use?

Standard two asks students to not only look for themes and ideas, but also the supporting details. Most students do not understand what a detail really is, much less analyze how details function. This chart gives students objective categories and examples that are easy to recognize. To create this chart, I write the name of each detail and a kid-friendly description on large sticky notes in advance. I simply have a discussion with my students about each detail, and then we add it to the chart.

Variations:

- This chart can be interactive and reusable. To do this, you need to make sure that your details and their descriptions are written on large sticky notes rather than the chart itself. Pull off all of the sticky notes and ask groups of students to reassemble the chart by matching the correct description to the detail.

- Remove the descriptions from the chart (leave the names of the details on the chart). Ask students to search online or look through a science or social studies textbook to find examples of each detail. When a student finds an example, he or she can write down the title of the text where they found it on a sticky note, and then add it to the chart.

- Students can also use this chart for writing. While they are writing, students can use this as a guide to develop their own details. You could even ask students to use and identify specific types of details throughout their writing.

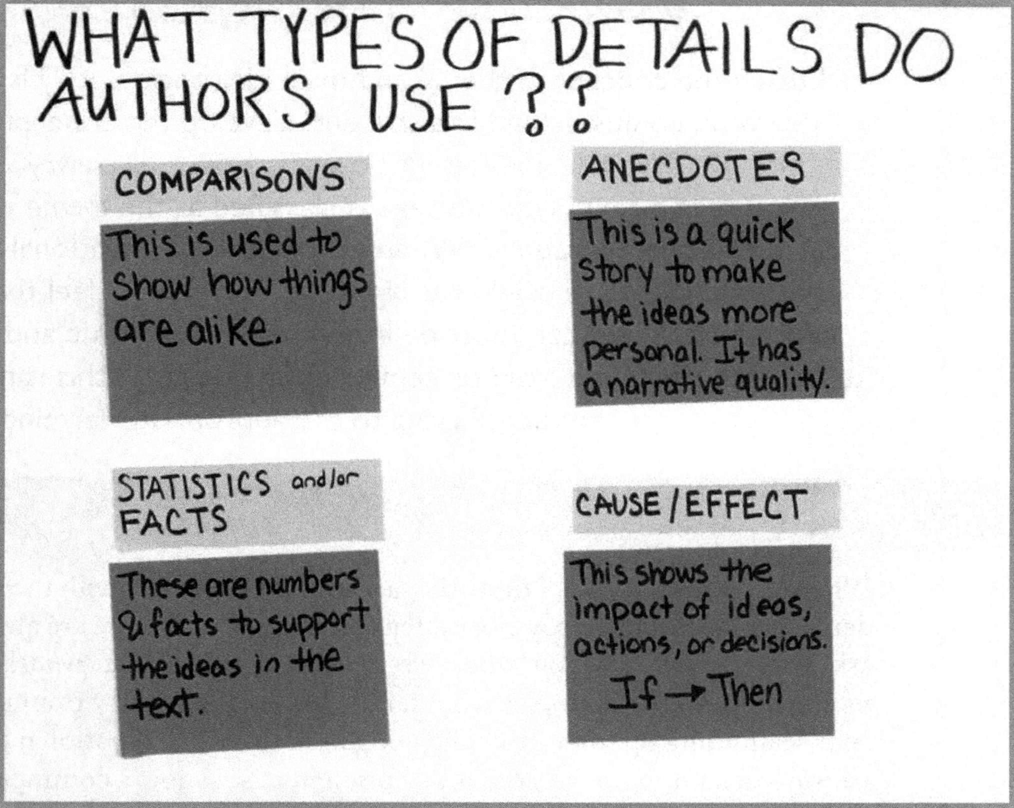

WHAT TYPES OF DETAILS DO AUTHORS USE ??

COMPARISONS

This is used to show how things are alike.

ANECDOTES

This is a quick story to make the ideas more personal. It has a narrative quality.

STATISTICS and/or **FACTS**

These are numbers & facts to support the ideas in the text.

CAUSE / EFFECT

This shows the impact of ideas, actions, or decisions.

If → Then

Figure 2.9 *What Types of Details do Authors Use?* chart

What's the Message?

I teach the concept of theme and main idea together. This cuts down on confusion and lets students develop the concept of a *message*. We talk a lot about how you have a *take-away* when you read a text. This message is classified as the *theme* when you are reading literature. When you shift to informational text, these messages are labeled as *big ideas*. Personally, I feel that an informational text can most definitely support a theme and that literature can reflect a main or central idea. I find that this is more about adhering to the appropriate terminology.

Introducing This Chart:

When I create this chart, I draw the face and write the text with the students. I ask students to pay close attention to the fact that we are always asking the same question when we read any type of text: *what's the message?* I provide examples from fairy tales for the literary examples, later scaffolding up to more challenging books. For informational text, I always default to my favorite tool: commercials. I show a commercial and ask students what the message or big idea is. AT&T commercials (found on YouTube) are great choices for this activity. The chart shown here was created with fourth graders.

Easy Fairy Tales and Fables to Reference:

1. "The Gift of the Magi"

2. "The Tortoise and the Hare"

3. "Cinderella"

4. "Little Red Riding Hood"

5. "Hansel and Gretel"

Figure 2.10 *What's the Message?* chart

Chapter 3

Connections & Interactions

Common Core Reading Anchor Standard 3:
Analyze how and why individuals, events, and ideas develop and interact over the course of a text.

	Literary Text	Informational Text
3rd	Describe characters in a story (e.g., their traits, motivations, or feelings) and explain how their actions contribute to the sequence of events.	Describe the relationship between a series of historical events, scientific ideas or concepts, or steps in technical procedures in a text, using language that pertains to time, sequence, and cause/effect.
4th	Describe in depth a character, setting, or event in a story or drama, drawing on specific details in the text (e.g., a character's thoughts, words, or actions).	Explain events, procedures, ideas, or concepts in a historical, scientific, or technical text, including what happened and why, based on specific information in the text.
5th	Compare and contrast two or more characters, settings, or events in a story or drama, drawing on specific details in the text (e.g., how characters interact).	Explain the relationships or interactions between two or more individuals, events, ideas, or concepts in a historical, scientific, or technical text based on specific information in the text.
6th	Describe how a particular story's or drama's plot unfolds in a series of episodes as well as how the characters respond or change as the plot moves towards a resolution.	Analyze in detail how a key individual, event, or idea is introduced, illustrated, and elaborated in a text (e.g., through examples or anecdotes).
7th	Analyze how particular elements of a story or drama interact (e.g., how settings shape the characters or plot).	Analyze the interactions between individuals, events, and ideas in a text (e.g., how ideas influence individuals or events, or how individuals influence ideas or events).
8th	Analyze how particular lines of dialogue or incidents in a story or drama propel the action, reveal aspects of a character, or provoke a decision.	Analyze how a text makes connections among and distinctions between individuals, ideas, or events (e.g., through comparisons, analogies, or categories).

Character Evolution

This chart is based on *The Wizard of Oz*. We had just read a version of this text and seen clips from the 1939 movie. I called students to our meeting area and we spent a few moments recapping what we remembered about the book and movie.

Introducing This Chart:

I began our discussion with a blank piece of chart paper with only the title written at the top. After initiating our discussion, I added the word *beginning* to the chart. I then called upon students to share what they remembered from the beginning. We repeated this for the middle and end. Then I placed *major events* and *character's response* on the chart. I added one sticky note under the beginning, referencing ideas that the students had just shared. I asked students to help me complete the middle and end sections. Having the summary conversation first helped my struggling students hear ideas and to develop their own ideas. Slowly, the more reluctant readers were able to join in on the conversation to confirm or reject their own understanding of the major characters and events.

Grade Level Considerations:

This chart was created with sixth graders. Standard three varies quite a bit by grade level, so examine the specifics for the grade that you teach. In the sixth grade, students are expected to describe how a particular dramatic plot unfolds and how the characters respond. This chart focuses specifically on events and how the characters respond to each of those events.

Being Interactive:

This chart is interactive and reusable. I created my beginning, middle, and end labels in advance on large 8"x6" sticky notes. These can all be removed and replaced with specific parts from the text. You can also easily change out the categories to focus on different elements.

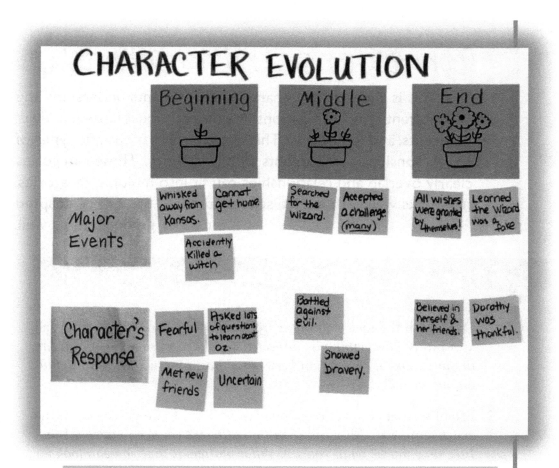

CHARACTER EVOLUTION

Beginning

Middle

End

Major Events
- Whisked away from Kansas.
- Cannot get home.
- Accidently Killed a witch
- Searched for the Wizard.
- Accepted a challenge. (many)
- All wishes were granted by themselves!
- Learned the Wizard was a Joke

Character's Response
- Fearful
- Asked lots of questions to learn about Oz.
- Met new friends
- Uncertain
- Battled against evil.
- Showed bravery.
- Believed in herself & her friends.
- Dorothy was thankful.

Figure 3.1 *Character Evolution* chart

Connections and Relationships

This is a key anchor chart to help students understand the different types of relationships that can exist between ideas, events, and individuals. This chart highlights specific types of relationships that students should look for. These categories clearly overlap and relationships can fit into multiple categories. This works well with middle school students, but can be adapted for other grade levels as well.

Introducing This Chart:

1. Open with the idea that there are relationships and connections all around us. *"Everything is connected or related in some way. You can literally make a connection between almost any two ideas, individuals, or events."*

2. Establish that connections don't always have to be perceived in the exact same way. *"Everyone can find different connections, too. What I see may not be what you see. What matters is that you can look for multiple connections and explain the relationships that you see."*

3. Explain that there are some common relationships between ideas, people, and events. I use eight different relationships with my students. You should expand or reduce the size of your list as needed.

4. Go through the list of relationship types and share a connection that you can make between real people, events, or ideas and ask for volunteers to do the same.

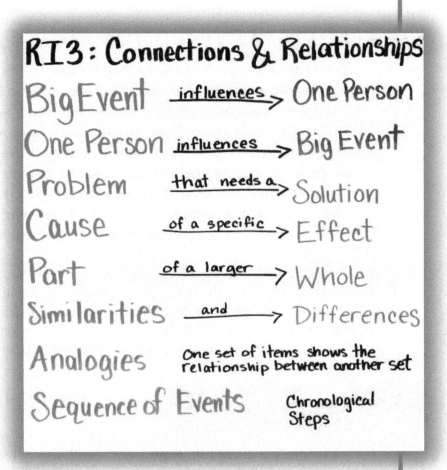

Figure 3.2 *Connections and Relationships* chart

Feelings, Motivations, Traits, Actions

This chart is an excellent resource to guide your third graders to think a bit deeper about the characters they encounter in literature. I like to write the categories on my chart in advance, but write the questions when I am with my students. I explain each category and question as I write it on the chart. It is a good idea to also have literature choices available that feature interesting or dynamic characters. Read excerpts from these examples to illustrate each category. I like to use picture books when I first introduce this chart. Later, after students have had more time to practice the skill, I switch to more complex text.

Grade Level Considerations:

This chart is specific to the demands of the third grade literature standard. Third graders are asked to describe characters in a story and how their actions contribute to the text. Because standard three varies quite a bit by grade level, you want to carefully examine the specifics for your grade level.

My Favorite Picture Books to Share:

1. *Stella Louella's Runaway Book* by Lisa Campbell Ernst
2. *Goldie Socks and the Three Libearians* by Jackie Mims Hopkins
3. *The Twits* by Roald Dahl
4. Any book with **Ramona** (Beverly Cleary) or **Fudge** (Judy Blume)
5. *If You Give a Pig a Pancake* by Laura Numeroff
6. *If You Give a Mouse a Cookie* by Laura Numeroff

Scaffolding Ideas:

1. For your struggling readers, this becomes a scaffold that allows them entry into the conversation about characters.

2. For your higher-achieving students, this offers a structure to organize their thoughts.

3. An easy variation is to focus on one or two categories at a time. Ask students to consider the impact of the characters' actions or just their character traits.

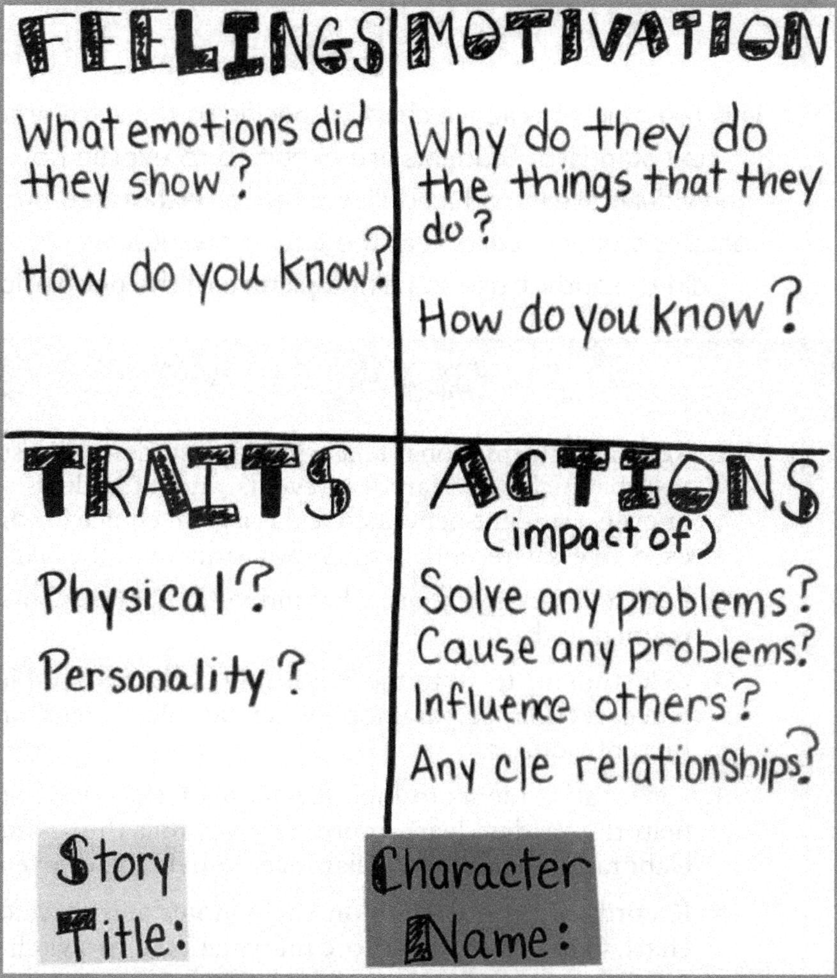

FEELINGS

What emotions did they show?

How do you know?

MOTIVATION

Why do they do the things that they do?

How do you know?

TRAITS

Physical?

Personality?

ACTIONS
(impact of)

Solve any problems?
Cause any problems?
Influence others?
Any c|e relationships?

Story Title:

Character Name:

Figure 3.3 *Feelings/Motivations/Traits/Actions* chart

Ideas, Events, Individuals

This reusable, interactive chart is specific to the sixth-grade informational text standard. Students are expected to explain how ideas, events, or individuals are introduced, illustrated, or elaborated upon in a text. This requires students to look at the text as a writer would. What strategies did the author use to paint a picture of the people, ideas, and events?

Teaching With This Chart:

1. Read an informational text with your students. Be sure to select a text that includes clear ideas, events, and individuals. A news article or even a student-generated text is a great choice for this activity. We used an essay recently written by a student in the class.

2. Lead a discussion about what individuals, events, and ideas are explained in the text.

3. Ask students to go to the beginning of the text and locate the sentence, section, or paragraph where an idea, event, or individual is first introduced.

4. Next, ask students to look for successive sections of the text that help the readers learn more. Explain that this is how the author elaborates on that particular idea, individual, or event.

5. Record this information on sticky notes and place on the anchor chart. Continue to add more information and switch out the sticky notes as you read other articles and essays.

Extensions:

1. Create a graphic organizer that mirrors this chart. Ask students to complete it when they read independently.

2. Scaffold this standard by focusing on just one concept: ideas, individuals, or events.

3. Ask students to use one of the same strategies in their own writing.

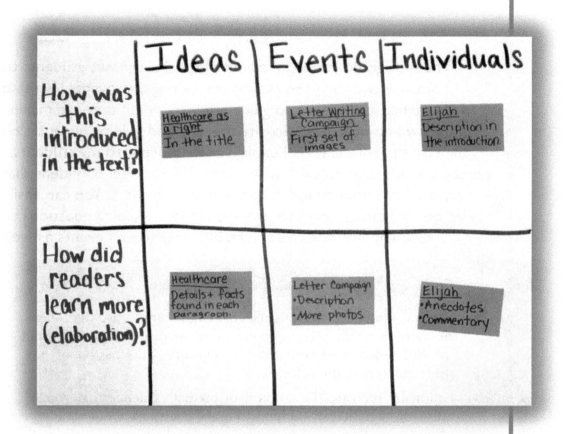

Figure 3.4 *Ideas/Events/Individuals* chart

Let's Compare

The fifth-grade literature standard specifically asks students to compare two or more characters, settings, or events. I create this chart as a reference to guide students when they are making their own comparisons. I write the title and guiding question on the chart in advance. As I explain each concept to my students, I record the information on a sticky note. When I feel confident that my students understand it, I place it on the chart. You can easily swap out the sticky notes to provide different guiding questions to examine not just characters, but settings and events as well.

Scaffolding Ideas:

- For your higher-level students, challenge them to use the categories here as headings or topics for more detailed paragraphs about the differences and similarities, including a discussion of how these differences impact the text.

- Gradually increase the amount of textual evidence that you require, or begin to ask students to make decisions about what type of evidence offers the *strongest* support for their assertions of similarity and/or difference.

Possible Literature Models:

1. *Blubber* by Judy Blume
2. *No Talking* by Andrew Clements
3. *Holes* by Louis Sachar
4. *Rikki-Tikki-Tavi* by Rudyard Kipling
5. *Loser* by Jerry Spinelli
6. *Sideways Stories from Wayside Schools* by Louis Sachar
7. *The Runaway Twin* by Peg Kehret

Figure 3.5 *Let's Compare* chart

Literary Interactions

This chart was created with seventh graders. The idea for the chart came from a collaboration with Andrea Battle, a fabulous middle school teacher working in Georgia. We were struggling with how to help students understand and write about how story elements interact. Asking simple questions about the characters or having students determine the story elements just seemed to fall flat. The rigor of this standard demands that students analyze *interaction* among story elements. We decided to quantify this and offer students some specific interactions to look for. Students were able to conceptualize just what an interaction was and gradually make decisions about the way that the story elements interacted to propel the ideas in the text.

Using This Chart:

We decided that familiar stories from fairy tales, fables, film, and television would be our starting point with students. Our goal was to help students make sense of the standard first. Once they conceptualized what we were asking them to do, we could bring in lengthier and more rigorous text.

Some of the first examples were from "Goldilocks and the Three Bears," *The Wizard of Oz*, and "Cinderella." Through conversations, we asked students to consider how the character traits of the wicked stepmother in "Cinderella" impacted the problems in the story, her choices, and the type of dialogue. Students discussed how these choices or problems would have been different if the stepmother was replaced with a different character, perhaps one with very different characteristics. Students began to consider how this could alter the rest of the story. From a discussion, we moved to writing, as a whole class, about the different interactions. I encouraged students to identify an interaction, and then explain the impact on the text. Students were able to write about interactions, shifting to more complex text later. You will notice that students quickly begin to understand what an interaction is and become excited about discussing their findings!

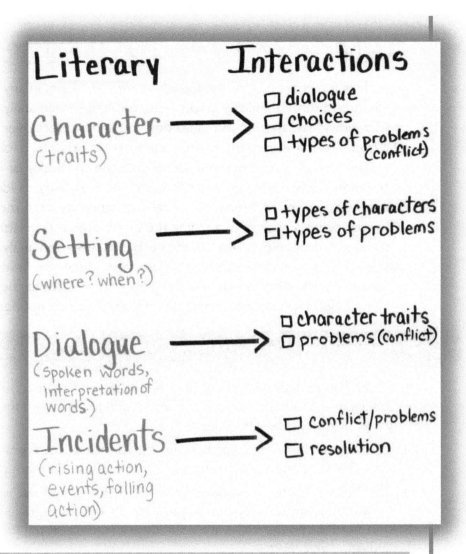

Figure 3.6 *Literary Interactions* chart

Where to Look for Connections

This fun chart can be the foundation for students in any grade level. Standard three explicitly states that students should analyze how and why individuals, events, and ideas develop and interact over the course of a text. At first glance this seems relatively simple. The problem is that after reading a text, many students struggle to classify or even define the individuals, events, or ideas in a text. This inability to identify these different categories of information prevents students from moving to the more complex task of examining the interactions. Your students need to be able to explore what an idea is before they can analyze how it is introduced or interacts with other elements. Once you have spent time discussing the distinctions, use the large sticky notes at the bottom to begin working on an analysis of how these components interact.

Grade Level Considerations:

1. When you prepare the title of this chart, the word *connection* should be replaced with either *relationship* or *interaction* to align with the exact language of your grade-level standard.

2. The large sticky notes at the bottom should include the types of interactions that your grade-level standard demands. Switch these out as needed.

3. Third-grade teachers should replace *ideas, events,* and *individuals* with *historical events, scientific ideas,* and *steps.* In the third-grade classroom, the questions on the sticky notes should ask students about *time sequence* and *cause and effect.*

4. Fourth-grade teachers should replace *ideas, events,* and *individuals* with *procedures, concepts/ideas,* and *events.* In the fourth-grade classroom, the questions on the sticky notes should ask students *what happened* and *why.*

5. Sixth-grade teachers should ask questions about *how these concepts were introduced, elaborated on,* or *illustrated.* The focus is on how the ideas, events, and people were presented and described to the reader.

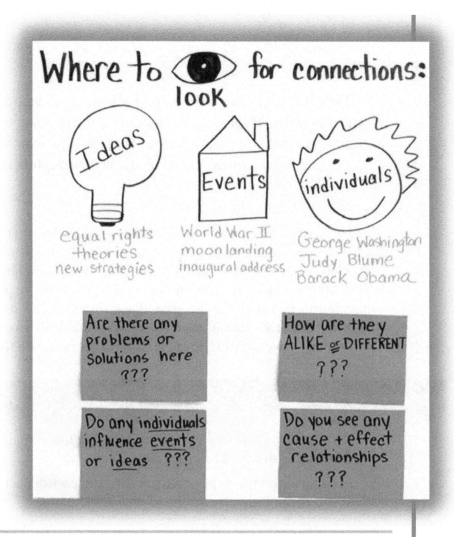

Figure 3.7 *Where to Look for Connections* chart

Why? Why? Why?

This chart supports the informational text standards for both third and fourth grade. When considering what type of text to choose, I tend to select sources that have a clear set of steps or move chronologically through historical events.

How to Use This Chart:

Read a passage from your social studies book or another informational text that sequences events. After you read the text, ask students to help select three of the major events. Write these events on large 8"x6" sticky notes. You may want to trim off the excess sticky note paper to make the information fit better on the step. Place them on the steps in sequential order. Students should then look for textual evidence to explain the causes of each event. Add the cause (reason) underneath the step (event).

Cross-Curricular Connections:

1. This chart is a great tool to help students examine a series of historical events in the social studies class.

2. This is an authentic opportunity to introduce students to cause-and-effect terminology.

3. Reinforce reading standard one by emphasizing how students are continuing to use textual evidence to support their thinking.

FUN!

When I teach social studies to fourth graders, we focus primarily on American history. I use this same chart to keep a class record of the events that we learn about and why they occurred. I like to start with five steps on a large bulletin board in the back of the classroom. By the end of the year, the butcher paper and additional steps easily reach the ceiling of our classroom!

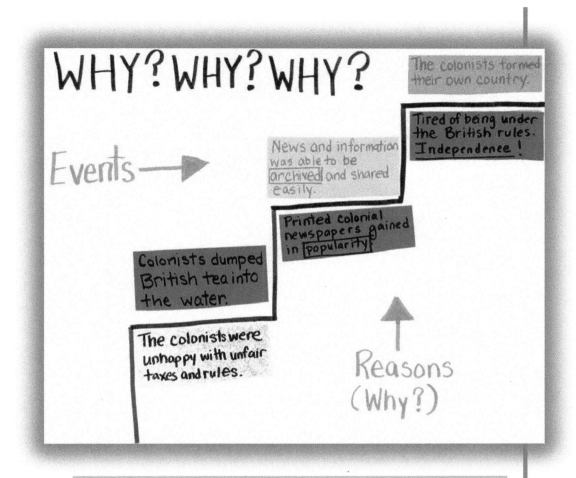

Figure 3.8 *Why? Why? Why?* chart

Chapter 4

Word Play

Common Core Reading Anchor Standard 4:
Interpret words and phrases as they are used in a text, including determining technical, connotative, and figurative meanings, and analyze how specific word choices shape meaning or tone.

	Literary Text	Informational Text
3rd	Determine the meaning of words and phrases as they are used in a text, distinguishing literal from non-literal language.	Determine the meaning of general academic and domain-specific words and phrases in a text relevant to a grade 3 topic or subject area.
4th	Determine the meaning of words and phrases as they are used in a text, including those that allude to significant characters found in mythology (e.g., Herculean).	Determine the meaning of general academic language and domain-specific words or phrases in a text relevant to a grade 4 topic or subject area.
5th	Determine the meaning of words and phrases as they are used in a text, including figurative language such as metaphors and similes.	Determine the meaning of general academic and domain-specific words and phrases in a text relevant to a grade 5 topic or subject area.
6th	Determine the meaning of words and phrases as they are used in a text, including figurative and connotative meanings; analyze the impact of a specific word choice on meaning and tone.	Determine the meaning of words and phrases as they are used in a text, including figurative, connotative, and technical meanings.
7th	Determine the meaning of words and phrases as they are used in a text, including figurative and connotative meanings; analyze the impact of rhymes and other repetitions of sounds (e.g., alliteration) on a specific verse or stanza of a poem or section of a story or drama.	Determine the meaning of words and phrases as they are used in a text, including figurative, connotative, and technical meanings; analyze the impact of a specific word choice on meaning and tone.
8th	Determine the meaning of words and phrases as they are used in a text, including figurative and connotative meanings; analyze the impact of specific word choices on meaning and tone, including analogies or allusions to other texts.	Determine the meaning of words and phrases as they are used in a text, including figurative, connotative, and technical meanings; analyze the impact of specific word choices on meaning and tone, including analogies or allusions to other texts.

Good Readers Use Context Clues

This chart is appropriate for all grade levels. While we teach vocabulary each year in school, students continue to struggle with how to determine the meaning of unknown words when they read. I like to give students explicit strategies to lean on when they get stuck and cannot make meaning of the text because of a tricky word.

How to Use This Chart:

I like to introduce the four strategies here one at a time. I find that students not only need to learn about a strategy, but they also need to have enough time to really practice the skill. I create this chart in front of my students by adding the title and the name of each strategy. Once I name the strategy, I place the sticky notes (pre-written) on the chart as examples. Next, I ask students to get up and go to their own book bins, our class library, or their textbooks. I have them locate a passage with either a visual, a specific word part, or a part of speech from the chart. We come back together and share our findings. Then, we talk about how different features help readers make meaning of the text or get through a tricky section of a book. We keep this chart pretty visible throughout most of the year. When students are stuck on a word or cannot make meaning, I help them use one of the strategies listed here.

Comma Sets:

Notice the term comma sets written under the category *Other Text*. I use this term to refer to descriptive clauses and appositive phrases. Neither of these parts of speech show up in the standards for students this young. Despite this, I find that the books that students read increasingly include more descriptive clauses and appositive phrases. Students struggle with this because it can seem very much like the words are out of place. Knowing the role that they play will help readers make meaning. This helps students recognize these types of phrases as descriptive.

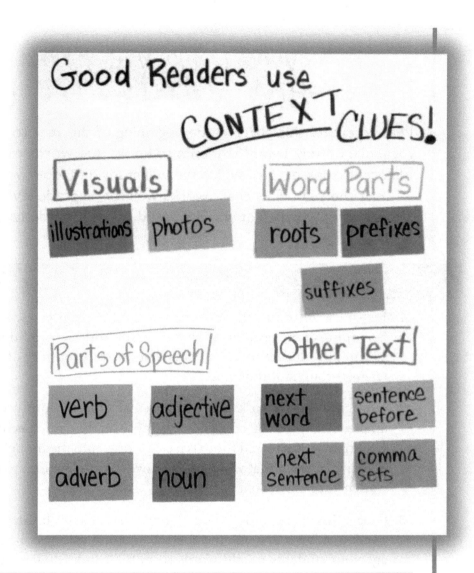

Figure 4.1 *Good Readers Use Context Clues* chart

What Do We Know About How Words are Used?

I like to create this chart at the beginning of the year to kick off our vocabulary study. I want students to know that words can play many different roles, each of which we will study and work with throughout the year. This chart works well for all grade levels. Vary the types of words that you list based on your grade-level standard.

Variations:

1. Instead of introducing all of the words at once, preview this at the beginning of the year with just one word. Add each additional word as you introduce it or as students demonstrate mastery of the other terms throughout the year.

2. Use this chart to work on one particular type of word use. For example, one week you could focus simply on domain-specific words. Use sticky notes to add those types of words into the thought bubble. When you finish that word study, move the sticky notes to the word wall in your classroom.

3. Create this chart to focus on different parts of speech: adverb, adjective, noun, verb, etc. Use the chart to add interesting words. Encourage your students to add words from their independent reading as well. This can double as a writing reference chart for students.

4. Turn this into an interactive chart for your students. Place your vocabulary words in the thought bubble. Ask students to sort them into student-selected categories. This can be written independently at their desks, or students can take the sticky notes off of the chart entirely to categorize them on the floor or wall.

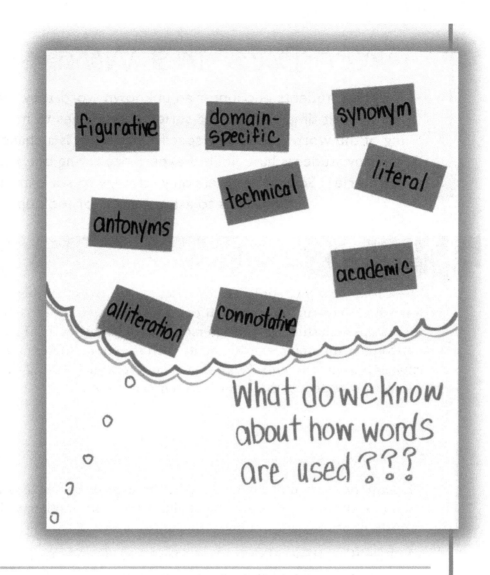

Figure 4.2 *What Do We Know About How Words are Used?* chart

What Does This Word Mean?

When students encounter an unknown word, they often have a difficult time trying out a series of strategies to make meaning of the word. Identifying specific strategies is a challenge, and many students have limited experience trying out a variety of strategies. Sometimes their only strategy to solve an unknown word is to ask someone or look up the word.

Introducing This Chart:

These four steps give students a clear set of directives that they can follow when they can't determine the meaning of a word. I like to share these steps with students as my personal set of strategies that I use when I encounter unknown words. I write each step in a different color and explain it to my students. Next, we try out the strategy using short text excerpts or sentences that I have written in advance.

Teaching Ideas:

1. Skip the chart altogether, and write the steps on sentence strips. Place these strips above the chalkboard or in another visible space.

2. Turn these steps into a student-friendly bookmark. Type up the steps in a cool font and print out copies for each student to put in his or her reading notebook for later reference.

3. Use your social studies or other content-area book to show students how they can use these strategies to learn all the time, not just during reading time. This works well because there are numerous unknown vocabulary words in content-area books.

What does this word MEAN?

① Read ahead to the end of the sentence to look for clues.

② Look for word parts to see what is familiar.

③ Think about the part of speech that the word is (adjective, verb...).

④ Replace the word with a "guess" word and see if it makes sense.

Figure 4.3 *What Does This Word Mean?* chart

Word Detectives

Often students cannot verbalize what they actually do to figure out unknown words. This is a simple visual to help them think about those strategies and remember to use them when they read independently. This particular chart was created with third graders.

Creating This Chart:

I draw this simple chart from start to finish in the classroom. I tell students that I want to share a few secrets that I use when I encounter an unfamiliar word in a book that I am reading. I really build this up as though these really are secret strategies that they are lucky enough to learn about. I explain one strategy at a time and write it on a large 8"x6" sticky note. I use a different color sticky note for each strategy. After each strategy is introduced, we talk about times when they may have used these strategies in the past.

Teaching Ideas:

- Select short passages to read aloud. As you read, model how you actually use each strategy. Think aloud and let students see you talk about and actively use the skill.

- If you teach younger students or students (of any age) that struggle with this standard, consider introducing one strategy per day. You could really spread it out over several days.

- Ask students to share their own strategies and add them to the chart as a growing resource for all readers.

Figure 4.4 *Word Detectives* chart

Word Play

Vocabulary instruction can be challenging. Students need a wide variety of tools and strategies to make sense of unfamiliar words. In addition to direct word study, I like to share universal strategies with my students and model how I use them when I get to complex or unknown words.

Grade Level Considerations:

If you are creating this chart with elementary school students, only list about five of the strategies. I find that this entire list can be overwhelming for younger students. For middle school students, I like to keep the full list intact.

Introducing This Chart:

I read aloud from an informational text or literature selection. I make sure to select one with several unfamiliar words. After I read the text, I go back and choose at least two of the words or phrases within the text. I ask students to help me think about what these words mean. I introduce each strategy and ask students to think about how that strategy might help me figure out the meaning of the unknown word. I explain that students should also try 1-2 of these same strategies when they read independently.

Teaching Ideas:

1. Introduce one or two of these strategies to your students each week.

2. Use a shared text to model, through a think-aloud, how to use each strategy.

3. Ask your students to create a modified Frayer model. Instead of using the traditional categories used with most Frayer models, let students use this list as a menu to choose what to include in each box.

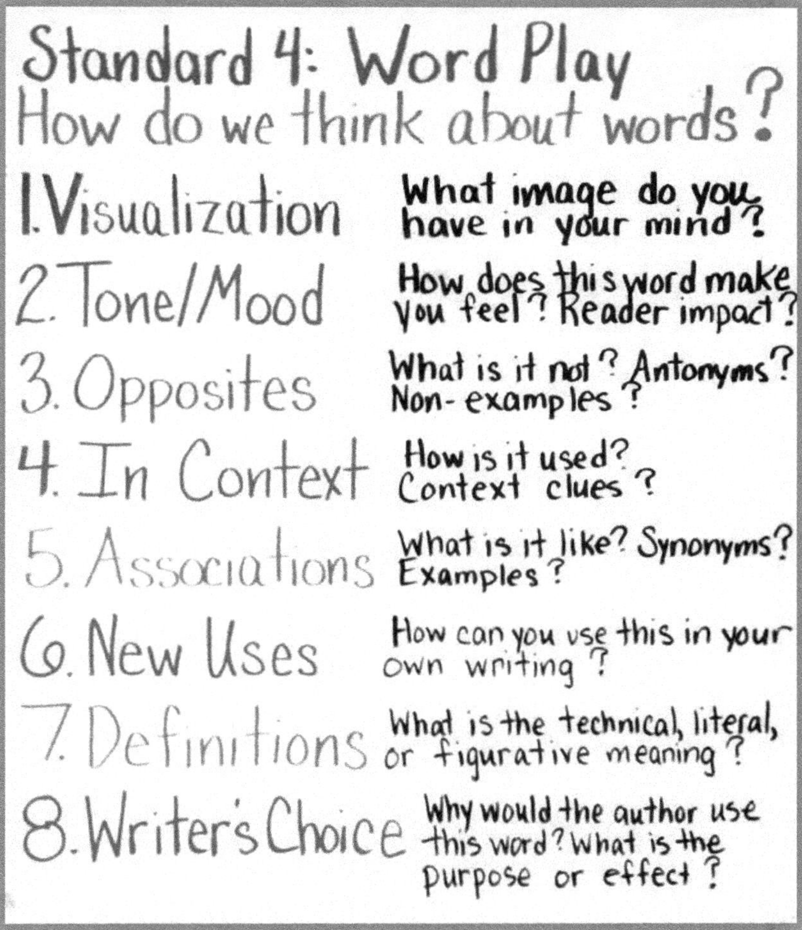

Standard 4: Word Play
How do we think about words?

1. Visualization — What image do you have in your mind?

2. Tone/Mood — How does this word make you feel? Reader impact?

3. Opposites — What is it not? Antonyms? Non-examples?

4. In Context — How is it used? Context clues?

5. Associations — What is it like? Synonyms? Examples?

6. New Uses — How can you use this in your own writing?

7. Definitions — What is the technical, literal, or figurative meaning?

8. Writer's Choice — Why would the author use this word? What is the purpose or effect?

Figure 4.5 *Word Play* chart

Chapter 5

Text Structure

Common Core Reading Anchor Standard 5:
Analyze the structure of texts, including how specific sentences, paragraphs, and larger portions of the text (e.g., a section, chapter, scene, or stanza) relate to each other and the whole.

	Literary Text	Informational Text
3rd	Refer to parts of stories, dramas, and poems when writing or speaking about a text, using terms such as chapter, scene, and stanza; describe how each successive part builds on earlier sections.	Use text features and search tools (e.g., key words, sidebars, hyperlinks) to locate information relevant to a given topic quickly and efficiently.
4th	Explain major differences between poems, drama, and prose, and refer to the structural elements of poems (e.g., verse, rhythm, meter) and drama (e.g., casts of characters, settings, descriptions, dialogue, stage directions) when writing or speaking about a text.	Describe the overall structure (e.g., chronology, comparison, cause/effect, problem/solution) of events, ideas, concepts, or information in a text or part of a text.
5th	Explain how a series of chapters, scenes, or stanzas fits together to provide the overall structure of a particular story, drama, or poem.	Compare and contrast the overall structure (e.g., chronology, comparison, cause/effect, problem/solution) of events, ideas, concepts, or information in two or more texts.
6th	Analyze how a particular sentence, chapter, scene, or stanza fits into the overall structure of a text and contributes to the development of the theme, setting, or plot.	Analyze how a particular sentence, paragraph, chapter, or section fits into the overall structure of a text and contributes to the development of the ideas.
7th	Analyze how a drama's or poem's form or structure (e.g., soliloquy, sonnet) contributes to its meaning.	Analyze the structure an author uses to organize a text, including how the major sections contribute to the whole and to the development of the ideas.
8th	Compare and contrast the structure of two or more texts and analyze how the differing structure of each text contributes to its meaning and style.	Analyze in detail the structure of a specific paragraph in a text, including the role of particular sentences in developing and refining a key concept.

Analyzing Literary Structures

There is such a strong connection between reading and writing. Most of the reading standards ask students not only to think about text, but to *write* about this thinking. This chart is a tool that helps students effectively write about their reading.

Creating This Chart:

To create this chart, you should draw the three steps ahead of time. I used a black marker and wrote on colored 8"x6" sticky notes. I cut them out into the shape of a cloud. If you do this, make sure that you write very close to the top of the sticky note. If you write in the middle, you will cut off all of the adhesive and need tape.

I told students that I wanted to teach them three steps that they should follow when explaining different literary structures. One by one, I stuck each cloud onto the chart. Next, I wrote the sentence frame with the students. When we finished, I asked them to use the frame to tell me about the structures in a book of their choice. The next day we shared the structures.

Variations:

- Teach each of the areas (identify, describe, and explain) as different lessons. Create one section at a time with your students, building this chart as you go.

- This chart can be transformed into a checklist, rather than a sentence or a paragraph frame.

- You can add additional sentences to require the inclusion of more textual evidence, or even specific types.

- This chart offers an organic way to scaffold and gradually release responsibility to your students. As students assume more responsibility for the task, they can develop their own paragraphs, being certain to include the necessary elements used here.

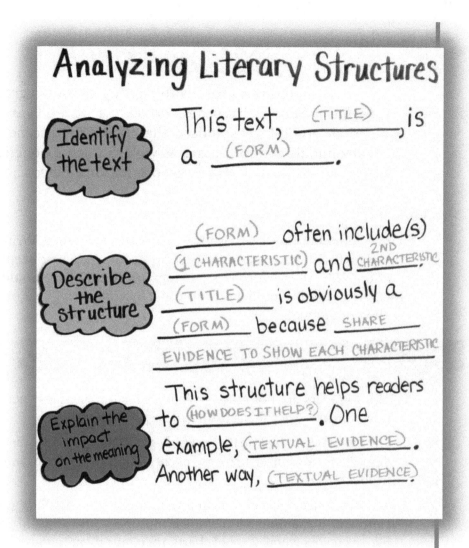

Figure 5.1 *Analyzing Literary Structures* chart

Deconstructing Text

I created this chart with a group of fourth graders using Seymour Simon's *Volcanoes*. While this worked very well with their grade-level standard, this chart has become a staple in many middle school classes as well. Students benefit from the visual representation of ideas and thinking.

Creating This Chart:

Draw your columns, each heading, and title in advance. Write all of the other text with your students as you introduce each concept. The last section, *How to Explain It,* is a paragraph frame. You should not only introduce this, but model how to use it by completing one of your own with your students.

Grade Level Considerations:

1. Third graders are not asked to look at the organizing structures with this standard. They focus primarily on text features.

2. The language of the fourth- and fifth-grade standard asks that students describe the overall structure of events, ideas, concepts, or information in a text.

3. The difference between fourth and fifth grade is that fifth graders are expected to examine and compare multiple texts. For fifth graders, I like to create several of these charts, then post them in the classroom or hang them on a chart stand. When your fifth graders move on to compare multiple texts, simply put two charts side-by-side to introduce the next step. If you go straight to comparison, your students will be lost.

4. In middle school, students are expected to analyze the structures and explain how the different components fit into the larger text. There is a chance that they will come to you without this exposure. This may be a great start before you delve into more complex levels of analysis with your middle school students.

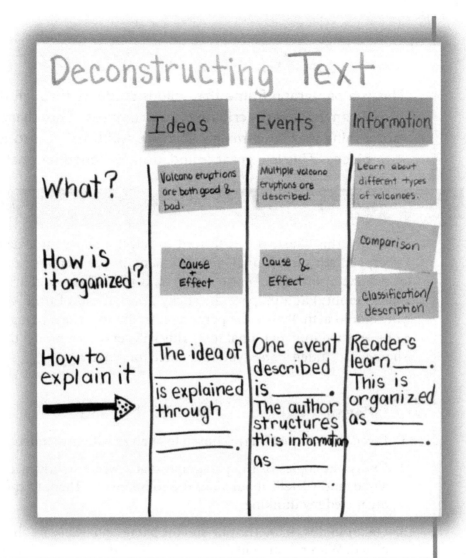

Figure 5.2 *Deconstructing Text* chart

Development Paragraphs

This is a paragraph frame that guides students through the process of naming and describing text structures. This chart helps take something that is seemingly abstract and break it into quantitative pieces. This is a great foundation for lengthier analysis of text.

Creating This Chart:

To create this chart, you will need to select a short informational text excerpt in advance. You also create many of the elements of this chart in advance. Write the entire paragraph frame on the chart (leave the blanks empty) and prepare the sticky notes ahead of time. Afterwards, you should actually use the paragraph frame to write a paragraph about your selected informational text. This will serve as a model that you can share with students after you introduce this chart.

Introducing This Chart:

1. I read the text that I have chosen to analyze with my students.

2. I pass out copies of the paragraph that I wrote in advance. I read it aloud, and we talk about all of the components. Then, I explain how I organized my thinking.

3. I take out this chart. The title and the paragraph frame are already completed. With my students, I write in what I did when I got to the blank spaces. I add: *describe the structure* and *explain the development* twice. I reference the paragraph that I wrote to reiterate how I followed this paragraph frame step by step.

4. The words *structures* and *development* are added at the bottom of the chart. This gives students not only a bank of different structures, but also a list of ways that authors can develop the text. I write these on sticky notes so that we can change them out as we learn more about development and structure.

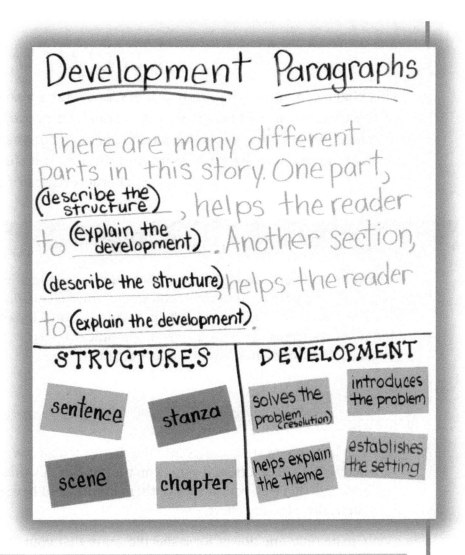

Figure 5.3 *Development Paragraphs* chart

Literary Text

This chart, created with fourth graders, provides a visual reminder of the three types of text listed in the standard: prose, poetry, and drama. Students are expected to differentiate between each one. Each flower represents a genre and the petals include different characteristics of each genre.

Creating This Chart:

I write the title and draw the flower pot on the chart in advance. I also go ahead and prepare my sticky notes. The other elements are created with my students. This can result in some very odd looking flowers, but it always seems like a group effort. The students also seem to have a stronger sense of ownership over "our" creation.

Variations:

- Cut large green sticky notes into the shape of petals. Write the characteristics of the different genres on the petals. Stick these onto your flowers. This way you can move them around and have a more aesthetically-pleasing chart.

- Create only one flower for a specific genre that your class is studying. If you do this, you would switch out your title and replace it with the name of that genre. Draw the other two charts (flowers) later in the year. Let students see how their knowledge of literary genres has blossomed!

- Not in the mood for flowers? This can become a simple checklist or you can draw three columns and label each one: *prose, poetry,* and *drama*. Under each category, list the different characteristics for each genre.

Figure 5.4 *Literary Text* chart

Name That Structure

This is a fun, effective chart to create when teaching the organizing structures found in informational text. Third graders really benefit from the strong visual representations of each structure. This is also a necessary building block for the analysis that they will do as they move into fourth and fifth grade.

Creating This Chart:

I write the title and divide the chart into four sections in advance. I write the descriptions on large 8"x6" sticky notes with the students. While I draw the illustrations with my students, I practice drawing them in advance. This makes it a lot easier to draw them quickly with your students.

Variations:

- Dreading the illustration process? Just reverse your definitions and illustrations. Draw your illustrations (or get someone else to) in advance on the large sticky notes, and write the definitions on the chart paper instead.

- Instead of adding all four structures, make individual charts for each structure as standalone elements. This will allow you to slowly introduce each type of structure throughout the year.

- Don't teach third grade, but have older students that don't understand the different structures? Create the chart with them as a reminder. Older kids like images, too! Middle school students can also create their own as a quick review of organizing structures!

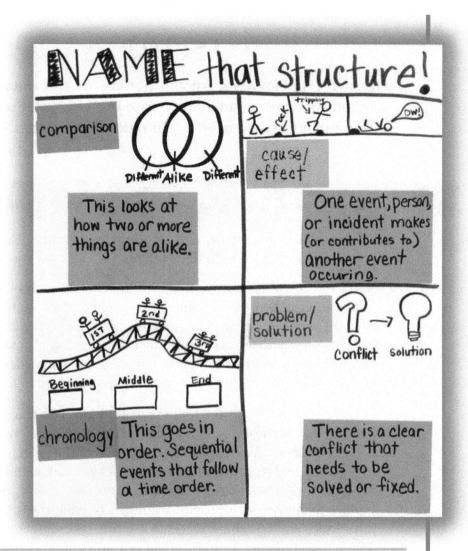

Figure 5.5 *Name That Structure* chart

Physical Structures

This chart is definitely most appropriate for elementary students. I worked with third graders to create this chart. Note: the focus in fourth and fifth grade is on organizational structures. Third graders will focus on physical structures.

Introducing This Chart:

1. I draw the columns, title, and headings in advance. The remaining information is added with the students.

2. Select informational text examples that illustrate each of the physical features. I usually rely on online news sources, or I photocopy a page from an anthology that shows one or more of the structures. I really enjoy using science books to introduce this standard. Science books are rich with graphics and multiple entry points for the reader. It is easy to do a quick scan and select an excerpt that is organized in multiple ways.

3. Read each of your selected text excerpts aloud with the students. After you read each one, discuss each type of structure. *What function did it serve? How does it work?* Classify each of the excerpts to the corresponding text structure and function. As you talk with the students, hand out large sticky notes to different students. Ask students to help explain the purpose or provide examples of what the different structures look like. For some sections, I wrote the characteristic myself. As much as possible, I used student examples to complete the chart.

Troubleshooting Tip:

When asking students to help draw examples, be sure to select multiple students to draw each structure. That way you can pick the most legible and accurate example. If you ask one student to illustrate the structure, there is always a chance that the illustration won't be recognizable.

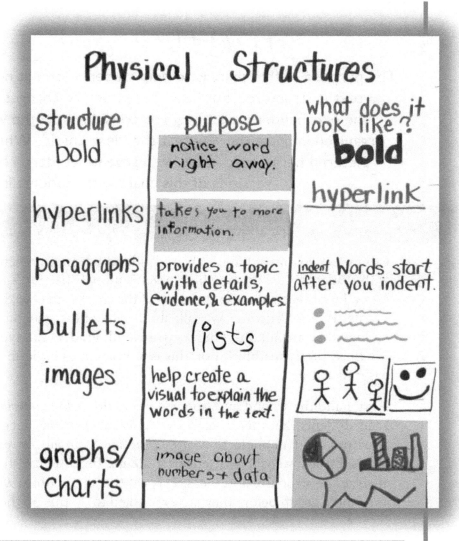

Figure 5.6 *Physical Structures* chart

Structure and Ideas

The purpose of this chart is to help students look at not only how a text is structured, but how that structure changes throughout the text. Students also begin to consider how the way a text is organized impacts the way that the ideas unfold. While the chart pictured here was created with seventh graders, I have created versions of this chart with students in grades 5-8.

Introducing This Chart:

I draw the columns, light bulb, and title in advance. When I sit down with students, I ask them which organizational structures they already know. I write each of these at the top of the chart with checkboxes. Then, I write: *Which Structure?* We talk about each of the structures, focusing on how they are alike and different. Seventh graders can typically identify these pretty readily. If not, this is a moment to back up and reteach basic structures.

Next, I add the second question: *How does this help to develop the ideas?* I tell students that this is really the So What? section. Recognizing the structure is not enough. *So what? What does it do for the reader?* Afterwards, I read a website article with students. Then, we use sticky notes to analyze the structure and ideas. I repeat this many times with students as a whole group before they are ever asked to do this on their own.

Free, Short, Online Articles:

1. **New York Times Archive** (1981-present) (http://query.nytimes.com/search/sitesearch/)

2. **Discover Magazine** (www.discovermagazine.com)

3. **Tween Tribune** (www.tweentribune.com)

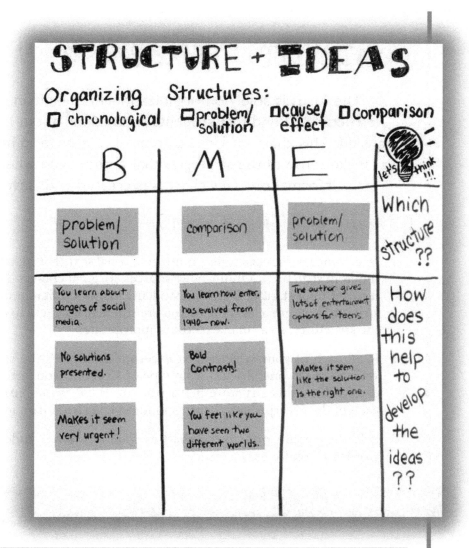

Figure 5.7 *Structure and Ideas* chart

Structure/Purpose/Signal Words

The focus is solely on organizational rather than physical text structures. I find that students rarely think about how a text is organized. This chart provides a point of reference to help students make sense of the strategies that authors use when organizing information. This chart was created with seventh graders.

Introducing This Chart:

1. In advance, select examples of informational text that match each of the different structures. Online news sources are great choices. For this lesson it is not important just yet that students identify different organizational structures within a larger text. You are still helping them to conceptualize the structures, so a small excerpt is appropriate.

2. Read each of your selected text excerpts aloud with the students. After you read each one, discuss what type of structure you notice. Be sure to discuss how this structure helps readers. *What is the purpose?* Classify each of the excerpts to the corresponding text structure and function.

3. Add the signal words to the chart as well. This gives students some key words to look for as they read.

Variations:

- You could create an individual chart for each structure. This can be ongoing throughout the year or taught as a longer unit that introduces each structure.

- Students could also create their own charts as you introduce and model each feature. This can easily become a personal reference chart for students to use when reading independently.

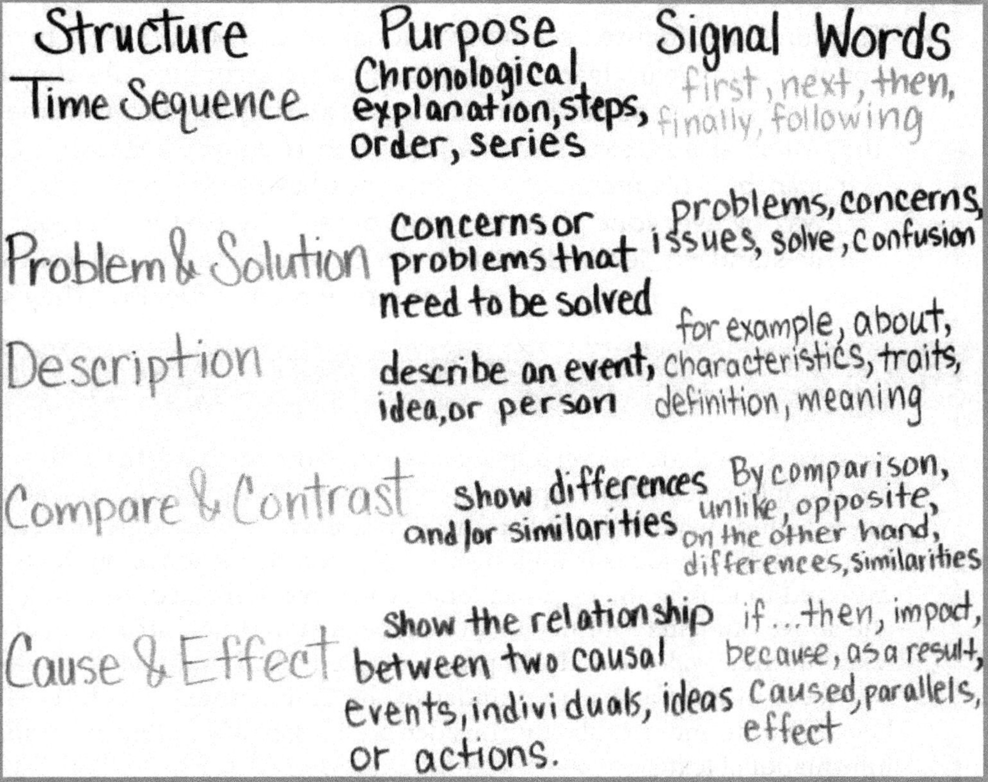

Structure	Purpose	Signal Words
Time Sequence	Chronological explanation, steps, order, series	first, next, then, finally, following
Problem & Solution	concerns or problems that need to be solved	problems, concerns, issues, solve, confusion
Description	describe an event, idea, or person	for example, about, characteristics, traits, definition, meaning
Compare & Contrast	show differences and/or similarities	By comparison, unlike, opposite, on the other hand, differences, similarities
Cause & Effect	Show the relationship between two causal events, individuals, ideas or actions.	if...then, impact, because, as a result, caused, parallels, effect

Figure 5.8 *Structure/Purpose/Signal Words* chart

Text Structure

This fun chart focuses on informational text. Students have probably spent several years learning about narrative structure. As they begin to learn more about informational text, they have to reframe how they think about text. Informational text is unique because it can be *nonlinear*. This means that it does not have to be read in the same way by everyone. Readers can "enter" the text in multiple ways. This standard demands that students recognize the different entry points and what function they serve.

Grade Level Considerations:

Each grade level focuses on a specific aspect of the standard. In third grade, for example, students are expected to understand the physical text features. These include hyperlinks, bullets, headings, sidebars, charts, graphs, etc. In fourth grade, the focus is no longer on physical text features; students are expected to look at the organizational structures of the text. In fifth grade and above, students continue to look at the organizational structures of the text, but they evaluate and compare multiple texts. I find that all students still seem to need a visual reminder of the different text structures. This helps them to more explicitly consider both types when they are reading informational text.

Creating This Chart:

1. Draw your umbrella in advance.
2. Explain to students that informational text can have multiple entry points or ways to get information. These entry points are the text structures, and these structures can be physical or organizational.
3. Write the two different areas on your chart: *physical text features* and *organizational structures/features.*
4. At this point you can share an example of each, discuss the characteristics, or have students locate examples from informational text in the classroom.
5. Due to the large number of features being added, you may want to introduce just a few each day.

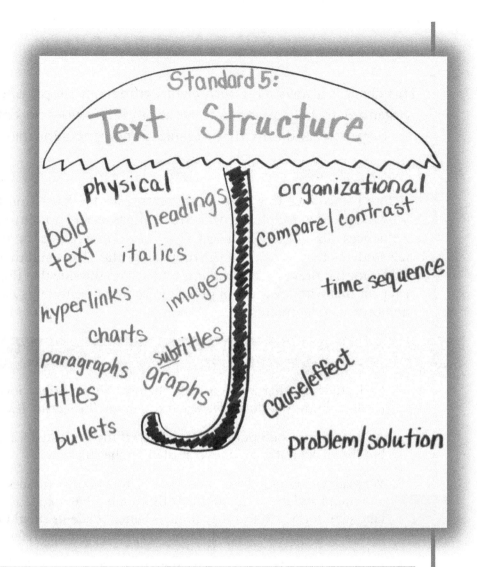

Figure 5.9 *Text Structure* chart

Text vs. Text

This chart is always a hit with eighth graders. It simply offers a visual organizer to help students think about how two different texts are organized and how that organization impacts meaning and style.

The Day Before:

Before I introduce this chart to students, I lead a discussion that I call: *This versus That*. I typically draw from sports, popular culture, or media influences. I might write: *Detroit Tigers or Atlanta Braves?* on the board. I tell students that one side of the room is for the Tigers and that the other side is for the Braves. I ask students to stand on the side that they support. I repeat this with a variety of other topics that my students have already demonstrated an interest in.

Introducing This Chart:

1. I ask students what we did the day before. After a brief conversation, I let them know that today we will learn about *Text versus Text*.

2. At this point, I pull out the chart. Everything is created for this chart, but the sticky notes are not yet posted on the chart.

3. We read two fractured fairy tales (yes, picture books), discuss the books, and then I add the sticky notes. At this point, I have students stand and take sides for which text they think is better. Students should physically choose sides just like they did with the popular culture references.

4. I call on students to share why they prefer a certain side. When they answer, I cheer and clap for the responses that answer the questions as written on the sticky notes. The students always get more excited about responding and try to make sure that their responses answer the questions as they are written.

5. I spend about a week beginning each class by reading increasingly complex pieces and repeating this activity. By the end of the week, we have graduated from picture books to excerpts of grade-level text.

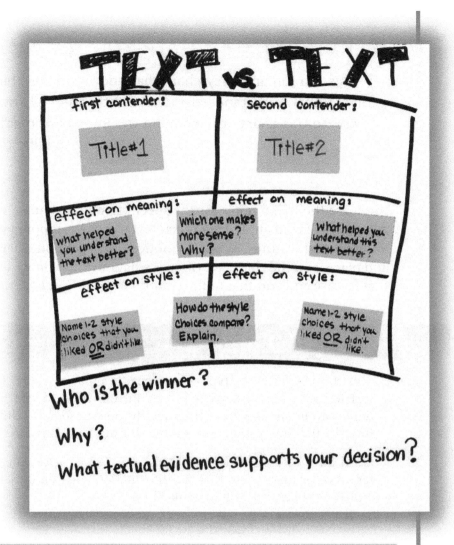

Figure 5.10 *Text Vs. Text* chart

Using Text Features

This is a fun and easy chart that addresses the third grade informational text standard. I use brightly-colored sticky notes to create this chart and examine the information gathered from specific text features.

Introducing This Chart:

I prepare the sticky notes for the specific features that we will study in advance. We read an informational text together, stopping when we see different text features. When we notice one, I pull out that sticky note and place it on the chart. We discuss what information we learned from that feature and add that to the column labeled *What I Learned*.

Teaching Tips:

1. This chart explores the types of information that we gather from specific text features. This activity is not an introduction to text features. Students should already have been taught how to identify different structures by the time you introduce this chart to your class.

2. Don't have colored sticky notes? Use one color sticky note, but use different color markers so that the information you add under the *Feature* and *What I Learned* columns matches.

Informational Text Sources:

1. Science and social studies books often feature a wide variety of text features. I like to select a two-page spread that we can look at together.

2. Websites also offer great choices for this activity. This will provide access to hyperlinks, animations, and multimedia features.

3. Consider writing your own informational text based on content that your students are studying.

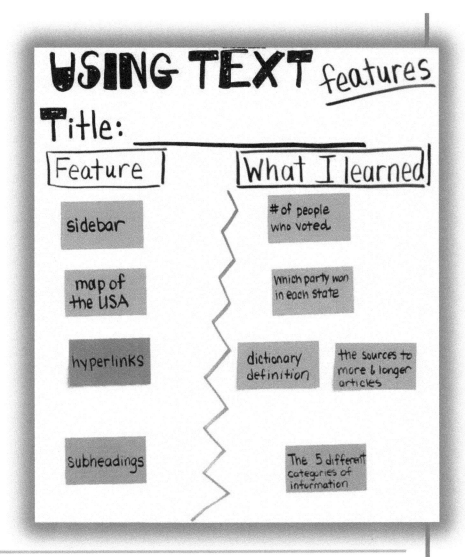

Figure 5.11 *Using Text Features* chart

Chapter 6

Point of View

Common Core Reading Anchor Standard 6:
Assess how point of view or purpose shapes the content and style of a text.

	Literary Text	Informational Text
3rd	Distinguish their own point of view from that of the narrator or those of the characters.	Distinguish their own point of view from that of the author of a text.
4th	Compare and contrast the point of view from which different stories are narrated, including the difference between first- and third-person narrations.	Compare and contrast a firsthand and secondhand account of the same event or topic; describe the differences in focus and the information provided.
5th	Describe how a narrator's or speaker's point of view influences how events are described.	Analyze multiple accounts of the same event or topic, noting important similarities and differences in the point of view they represent.
6th	Explain how an author develops the point of view of the narrator or speaker in a text.	Determine an author's point of view or purpose in a text and explain how it is conveyed in the text.
7th	Analyze how an author develops and contrasts the points of view of different characters or narrators in a text.	Determine an author's point of view or purpose in a text and analyze how the author distinguishes his or her position from that of others.
8th	Analyze how differences in the points of view of characters and the audience or reader (e.g., created through the use of dramatic irony) create such effects as suspense or humor.	Determine an author's point of view or purpose in a text and analyze how the author acknowledges and responds to conflicting evidence or viewpoints.

Author's POV

This chart is a great introduction to point of view. The questions included on this chart are not exhaustive, but are meant to provide students with several entry points for thinking about point of view. Every grade level can benefit from this type of chart.

Introducing This Chart:

1. Write *Author's Point of View* on the chart. Ask students what they think the term means. Have a discussion and let students talk it through.

2. Explain that you want to share a few questions that can help students think about point of view. *"There are a few questions that will help you think about the author's point of view. We are going to record them here, so that you can refer to them as we talk more about point of view."*

3. Add each question, one at a time. Emphasize that these questions all ask the same thing, but use different words. They are just there to help students think about the author and his or her views as they read a text.

4. Add the key words listed at the bottom of the chart. Tell students that these are the type of vocabulary words that they should use when they discuss point of view.

Practicing With Students:

1. Read an informational text excerpt aloud. I like to use a short picture book, website excerpt, movie review, letter to the editor, or news article.

2. Ask students to think about the author's point of view as you read. *"As I read this aloud, I would like for you to ask yourself the questions listed on our anchor chart to see if you can come up with an answer. Be prepared to provide textual evidence to support what you think."*

3. Call on different students to answer one of the questions from the chart about that text. Encourage students to point out evidence from the text that helped them infer the point of view.

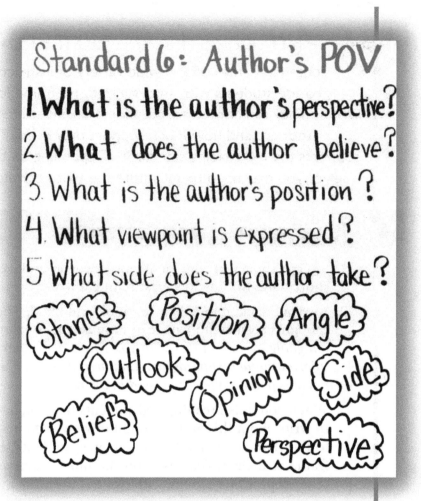

Figure 6.1 *Author's POV* chart

Author's POV Sentence Frames

Sentence frames offer a wide variety of instructional options. They provide students with an organizational frame for their reading and writing. They can also be adapted for different students based on where they are and how much support they need. This sentence frame supports the 6-8 reading standards. Depending on the type of text you select, you may need to substitute the word *narrator* in place of *author*.

Introducing This Chart:

1. Select a short text with an obvious view point. I like to read one of the short "One-Minute Reviews" found at www.rogerebert.com.

2. As you read, remember to think out loud, sharing questions or thoughts so that students can have access to your inner dialogue. *"I am going to share a text with you where an author has written a short informational text paragraph that describes a movie. The author has an obvious point of view expressed in the text."*

3. When you finish reading, tell students that you have a really easy way to write about this author's point of view. Add one sentence at a time to the chart. As you add the sentence, students should complete the frame at their desks, based on the movie review that you have just read. Repeat this activity with two to four more movie reviews.

Increasing the Rigor:

- Select a new text that is longer and more complex.

- For seventh and eighth graders it is important to eventually move up to pieces that acknowledge a counterargument.

- Encourage students to add additional sentences or create a more detailed frame that they can share with the class. You will be surprised at the variety of ideas that emerge here.

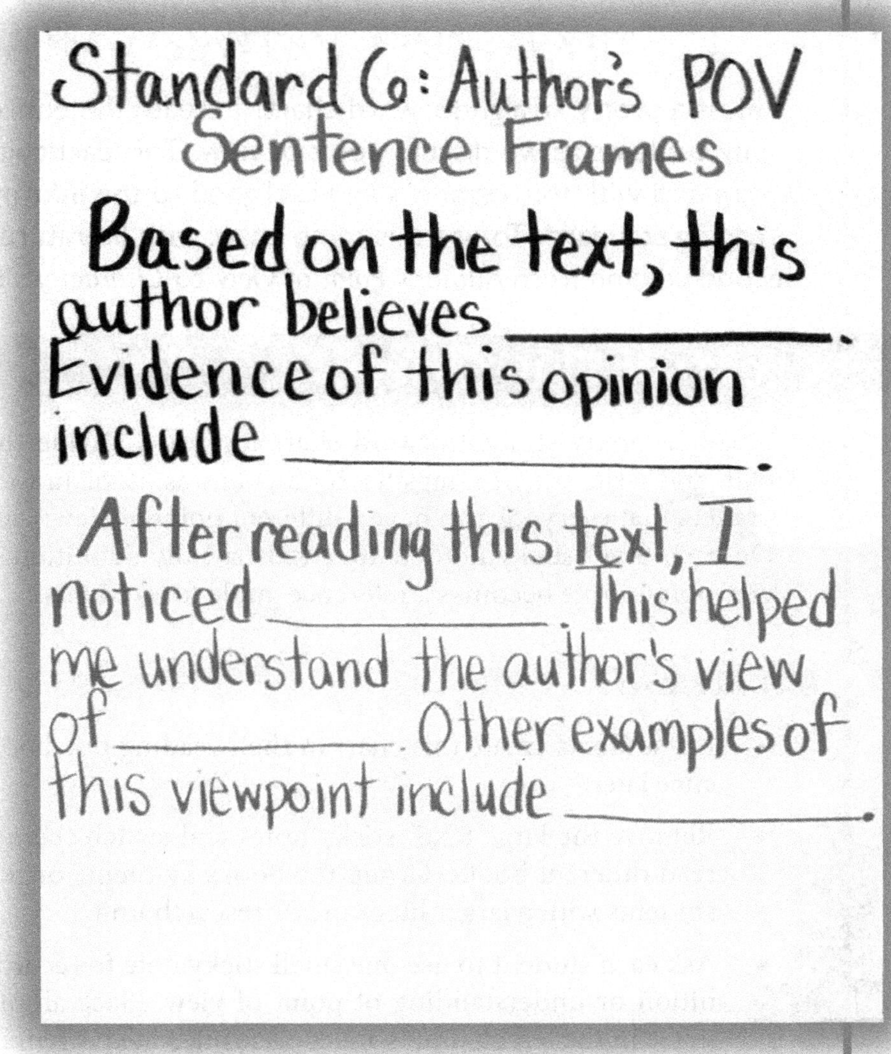

Standard 6: Author's POV Sentence Frames

Based on the text, this author believes _____.
Evidence of this opinion include _____.

After reading this text, I noticed _____. This helped me understand the author's view of _____. Other examples of this viewpoint include _____.

Figure 6.2 *Author's POV Sentence Frames* chart

Distinguishing Between Viewpoints

This is a pretty straightforward chart. I create the entire chart with my students as we discuss point of view. This particular chart was created with third graders and is aligned to the informational text reading standard. To use this same chart with literature, change the second column from *Author's Point of View* to *Character's Point of View*.

Creating This Chart:

This is a pretty straightforward chart to create. Divide the chart in half, and write the headings for both columns. Explain to your third graders that everyone can have a different point of view, even authors. On each 8"x6" sticky note, write a kid-friendly definition of the two viewpoints. This becomes a reference guide for students.

Variations:

- Let students create this chart in their reading notebooks to reference later.

- Remove the large 8"x6" sticky notes and switch them out as you read different books. Group the books by theme or topic to help students with a larger literature or research unit.

- Ask each student to use one small sticky note to record their definition or understanding of point of view. Place all of the sticky notes in the left column so that everyone's idea is represented.

Double Duty:

Once students move beyond the basics, this chart is transformed into an interactive chart. Use this regularly to compare different points of view as your class reads different books. Using sticky notes, rather than writing directly on the chart, is essential for this purpose.

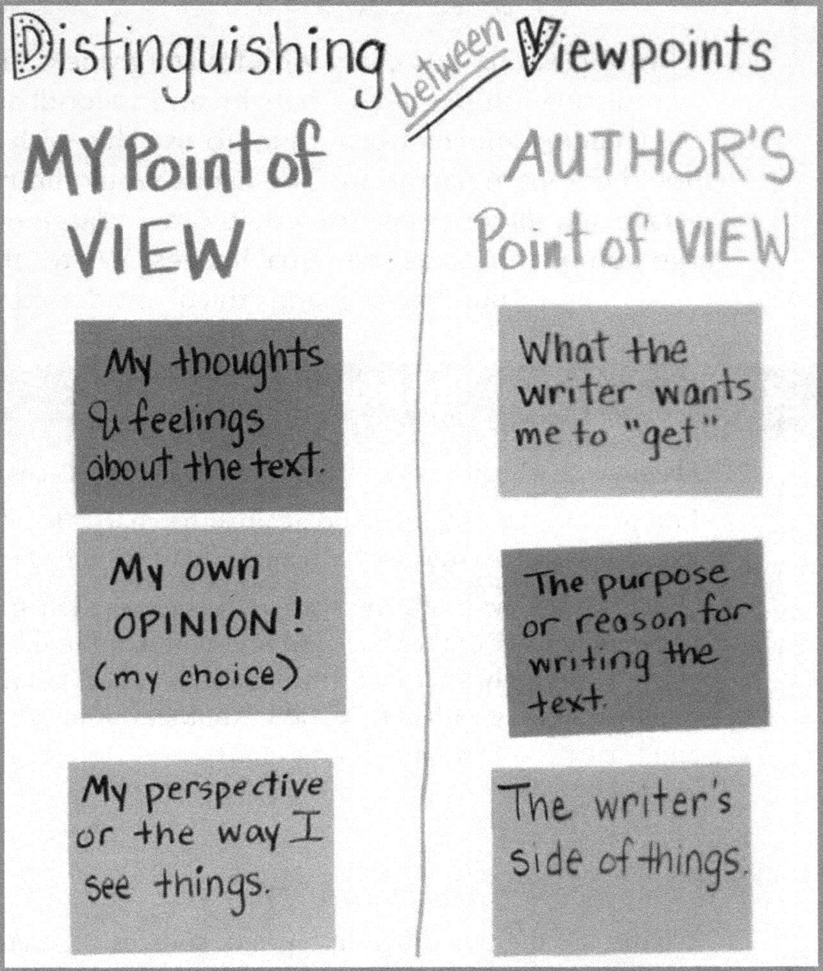

Figure 6.3 *Distinguishing Between Viewpoints* chart

Firsthand or Secondhand

I love creating this chart with fourth graders. This chart is used to distinguish between firsthand and secondhand sources when reading informational text. To use this with literary text, you should compare narration. The hands would be replaced with *first person* and *third person*. You could draw a large number one and a large number three as the visual images. Write "first" inside of the number one and "third" inside of the number three.

Creating This Chart:

1. I begin with a blank chart. I like to create all of the pieces with my students.

2. I do practice tracing my hand against the chart a few times beforehand just to get used to the awkward angle that I will need to draw from.

3. When I sit down with my readers, I trace my left hand in the upper left-hand corner of the chart and my right hand in the lower right-hand corner. This is always a bit awkward and crooked, but the kids are always quietly watching with anticipation. Another option is to call on a student and trace his or her hand on the chart.

Introducing This Chart:

1. We discuss the two different types of sources (firsthand and second-hand) and add the characteristics of each on colored sticky notes.

2. After this introduction, I read as many text excerpts as I can aloud. After each one, I ask students to help me classify excerpts as firsthand or secondhand. If we are using literature, I ask them to determine if the narration is written in first person or third person.

3. Once they make a decision, I ask students to touch the sticky note with the characteristic that helped them classify the source. We repeat this as many times as possible.

Figure 6.4 *Firsthand or Secondhand* chart

Outside/Inside Clues

Outside/Inside is such a useful chart for readers. It is interactive and helps students understand that they can explicitly pull out excerpts from the text and make inferences about the author's point of view. When you create this chart with students, they should already have been introduced to the concept of point of view. This chart will help students to move beyond mere identification. Notice that students are working not just on standard six, but they are also integrating the skills of standard one. Textual evidence and inferences work together when analyzing text. This particular chart was created with sixth graders, but can be adapted for all grade levels.

Creating This Chart:

1. I drew the images in advance by looking online at cartoon pictures of a living room and of a landscape.

2. When I sat down with my readers, I asked them what they thought the images represented. After a brief discussion, I recorded the words *outside* and *inside* on the chart.

3. I explained that clues on the *outside* help you make decisions about the *inside*. For this chart, we revisited two different articles about Black Friday shopping.

4. Together, we determined each author's viewpoint about Black Friday. These viewpoints and the textual evidence were recorded on large 8"x6" sticky notes.

Keeping the Focus:

This inevitably becomes a discussion of stereotypes and assumptions as well. I want students to understand that I am not looking for the same cookie-cutter inferences. What I am interested in is that they can provide me with textual evidence to support their inferences about the author's point of view.

Outside | Inside

Look for <u>outside</u> clues to make inferences about the author's point of view!!

What we read: | **Author's POV:**

"people recklessly shoved their way into the store consumed by greed for more things."

The author has a negative attitude towards Black Friday sales.

"As soon as the doors swung open, happy shoppers eagerly dashed in to look for deals."

The author is excited about Black Friday. Very positive.

Figure 6.5 *Outside Inside Clues* chart

Three Pieces of the Author POV Puzzle

This anchor chart was created with seventh graders, but is appropriate for all middle school students. When students are asked to analyze how an author develops point of view, they really don't know what they should be looking for. Content, structure, and word choice are three clear categories for students to frame their thinking around. I explain to students that these three areas are all pieces of the puzzle. Each one is important in a different way.

Creating This Chart:

1. I draw my three puzzle pieces in advance. A quick internet search for "puzzle pieces" will yield hundreds of examples to help you see the angles and variations for your own illustration.

2. When I talk with my readers, I write the words *content, structure,* and *word choice* on each puzzle piece as I introduce them.

3. I write the different characteristics or questions on the sticky notes as we discuss them. I trim the sticky notes to fit as many as possible on the chart.

4. Be sure to use sticky notes (and not write directly onto the chart) so that you can switch out the characteristics or add to them. These characteristics may change depending on whether you are reading literature or informational text.

Writing Connection:

Ask students to create a simple, four-sentence paragraph to analyze point of view. First, students should state what they believe is the author's point of view. Then, they can reply to one of the questions listed under the content puzzle piece. Next, students select a structure from the next puzzle piece that supports their statements. Finally, students should add a sentence from the *word choices* section. This can also be extended to include additional textual evidence.

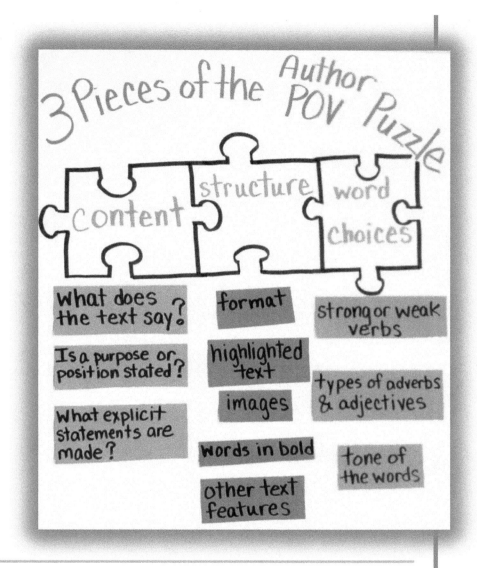

Figure 6.6 *Three Pieces of the Author POV Puzzle* chart

Chapter 7

Beyond Text

Common Core Reading Anchor Standard 7:
Integrate and evaluate content presented in diverse formats and media, including visually and quantitatively, as well as in words.

		Literary Text	Informational Text
3rd		Explain how specific aspects of a text's illustrations contribute to what is conveyed by the words in a story (e.g., create mood, emphasize aspects of a character or setting).	Use information gained from illustrations (e.g., maps, photographs) and the words in a text to demonstrate understanding of the text (e.g., where, when, why, and how key events occur).
4th		Make connections between the text of a story or drama and a visual or oral presentation of the text, identifying where each version reflects specific descriptions and directions in the text.	Interpret information presented visually, orally, or quantitatively (e.g., in charts, graphs, diagrams, time lines, animations, or interactive elements on Web pages) and explain how the information contributes to an understanding of the text in which it appears.
5th		Analyze how visual and multimedia elements contribute to the meaning, tone, or beauty of a text (e.g., graphic novel, multimedia presentation of fiction, folktale, myth, poem).	Draw on information from multiple print or digital sources, demonstrating the ability to locate an answer to a question quickly or to solve a problem efficiently.
6th		Compare and contrast the experience of reading a story, drama, or poem to listening to or viewing an audio, video, or live version of the text, including contrasting what they "see" and "hear" when reading the text to what they perceive when they listen or watch.	Integrate information presented in different media or formats (e.g., visually, quantitatively) as well as in words to develop a coherent understanding of a topic or issue.
7th		Compare and contrast a written story, drama, or poem to its audio, filmed, staged, or multimedia version, analyzing the effects of techniques unique to each medium (e.g., lighting, sound, color, or camera focus and angles in a film).	Compare and contrast a text to an audio, video, or multimedia version of the text, analyzing each medium's portrayal of the subject (e.g., how the delivery of a speech affects the impact of the words).
8th		Analyze the extent to which a filmed or live production of a story or drama stays faithful to or departs from the text or script, evaluating the choices made by the director or actors.	Evaluate the advantages and disadvantages of using different mediums (e.g., print or digital text, video, multimedia) to present a particular topic or idea.

Evaluate Different Mediums

Students seem to really struggle when asked to compare specific texts from various mediums. This chart was created with eighth graders, but every grade level could benefit from a visual that helps establish the value (and shortcomings) of each medium.

Creating This Chart:

1. I wrote the different mediums (formats) on large sticky notes, then cut them down to size. You can write your mediums on shapes, plain sticky notes, or even colored paper, and tape them onto the chart.

2. For each medium, I shared an example with students. We held a discussion about what was effective and what was challenging. After this discussion, we recorded the pros and cons on this chart.

3. Later on in the year, when students begin to analyze different types of text, this chart can be used as a reference.

Connecting School and Home:

In school, students primarily rely on printed text. The irony is that most students gather information for their personal learning (which they value) from digital, multimedia, and video sources. There seems to be an unspoken hierarchal relationship that classifies print sources as academic and everything else as secondary. This chart helps bridge the gap between school and home, while pointing out the value of each medium.

Variations:

- Switch out the mediums (formats) listed here for different ones, based on your grade-level standard (drama, poetry, audio).

- Instead of looking at general formats, replace the categories with specific texts. For example, the transcript of Dr. King's "I Have a Dream" speech, the audio of the same speech, and the video of the same speech. Have students compare the impact and differences in the columns.

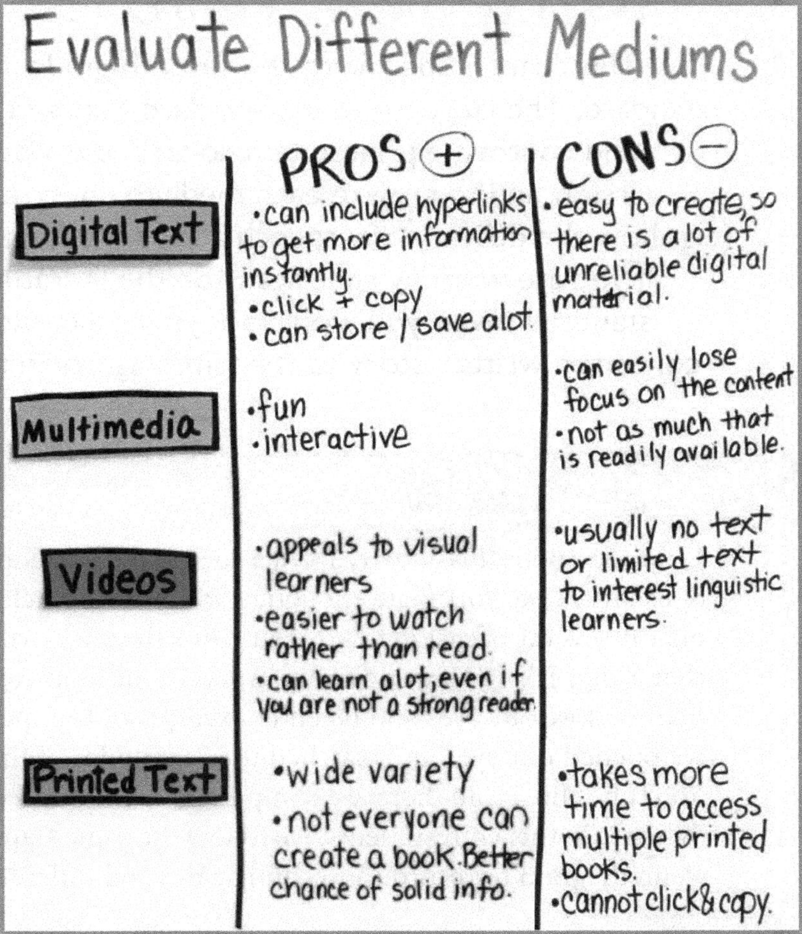

Evaluate Different Mediums

PROS ⊕   CONS ⊖

	PROS ⊕	CONS ⊖
Digital Text	• can include hyperlinks to get more information instantly. • click + copy • can store / save a lot.	• easy to create, so there is a lot of unreliable digital material.
Multimedia	• fun • interactive	• can easily lose focus on the content • not as much that is readily available.
Videos	• appeals to visual learners • easier to watch rather than read. • can learn a lot, even if you are not a strong reader.	• usually no text or limited text to interest linguistic learners.
Printed Text	• wide variety • not everyone can create a book. Better chance of solid info.	• takes more time to access multiple printed books. • cannot click & copy.

Figure 7.1 *Evaluate Different Mediums* chart

How Do These Formats Compare?

This chart is specific to the seventh-grade informational text standard. The language of the standard asks students to compare and contrast a printed text to an audio, video, or multimedia version, and to analyze each medium's portrayal of the subject (e.g., how the delivery of a speech affects the impact of the words). If you are working specifically on the literature component of standard seven, you would ask your students to compare and contrast a written story to the film, stage, or multimedia version.

Teaching Ideas:

I learned about this activity from a social studies School Improvement Specialist. I was fortunate enough to witness her teaching this to teachers on several occasions. We read from the transcript of Martin Luther King, Jr.'s "I Have a Dream" speech out loud together. Next, she had us close our eyes and listen to excerpts of the speech. Afterwards, we opened our eyes and watched the remainder of the footage from a YouTube clip. From there, we compared and contrasted the differences. When I do this with students, we follow the same steps, but we add the Venn diagram to record those similarities and differences.

Sources for Video, Audio, and Written Speeches:

1. **PBS Website** (www.pbs.org)
There are tons of videos and articles here, organized by subject area.

2. **American Rhetoric** (www.americanrhetoric.com)
This website has a wide variety of speeches. You can download over a hundred transcripts and audio files.

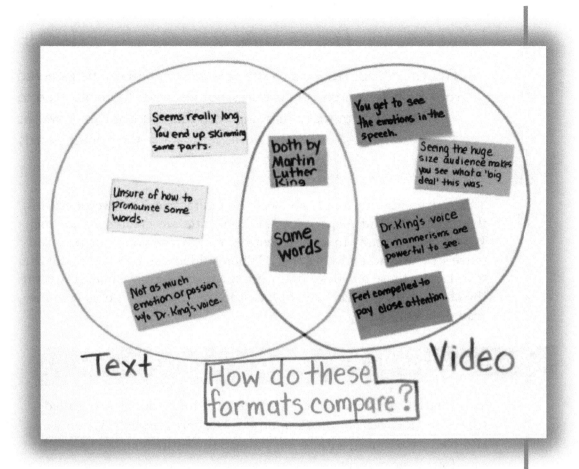

Figure 7.2 *How Do These Formats Compare?* chart

Learning from Words and Visuals

This chart helps students to see how information can be gathered from multiple sources and features, not just text. Students need to consider how to make meaning from the text features as well as the printed words.

Creating This Chart:

This chart is reusable and can easily be interactive. The two questions, the chart title, and a space for the book title are created in advance. When you are ready to use this with a book, write your title on a sentence strip and add it to the chart. When students share ideas about the text, I write these on sticky notes. After a discussion, we place them on the chart in the correct category. I swap out the sticky notes when we read different books.

Informational Text Featured Here:

This chart was created after reading an informational text called *Chocolate: Riches from the Rainforest* by Robert Burleigh. When we completed this chart, we had not yet read the entire text. We focused on a four-page excerpt.

This colorful book uses captions, bold print, timelines, drawings, and photographs to detail the history of chocolate. Tracing the origins of chocolate historically, the text includes references to the Aztecs, slavery, rainforests, and the cacao tree. There is a good balance of serious, historical details and fun, modern facts. Readers study a bevy of fun topics from Milton Hershey to the Tootsie Roll factory.

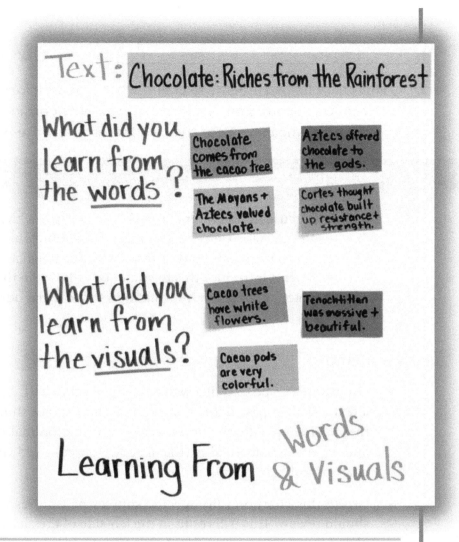

Text: Chocolate: Riches from the Rainforest

What did you learn from the words?

Chocolate comes from the cacao tree.

Aztecs offered chocolate to the gods.

The Mayans + Aztecs valued chocolate.

Cortes thought chocolate built up resistance + strength.

What did you learn from the visuals?

Cacao trees have white flowers.

Tenochtitlan was massive + beautiful.

Cacao pods are very colorful.

Learning From Words & Visuals

Figure 7.3 *Learning from Words and Visuals* chart

My Learning

This chart helps students examine what type of information they can learn from different formats. Students consider how they make meaning from the text features and the written text.

Creating This Chart:

This chart is reusable and interactive. You simply divide the chart paper in half. Each side has a title and a subtitle. The subtitles are really guiding questions to help your readers think and clarify what fits into each category. When I introduce this to students, I like to do the writing on the sticky notes and add the information as we discuss our reading.

Variations:

- Use painters' tape to split a wall or chalkboard in half. After you read a text together, pass out two sticky notes to pairs of students and let them come up with one new piece of information that they learned and where they learned it (the specific source). Add these to your chart or wall.

- Create this chart and list specific sources or features that students should review. This will result in the left side of the chart being completed by you. Assign each student a specific feature or source. Then, ask students to record what they learned from each source on the chart. You could also reverse this and ask students to determine where the information is located in the text.

- Ask students to simply fold a sheet of notebook paper in half and label each side to match this chart. As they read independently, ask them to record the specific information that they learn and where they learned it from.

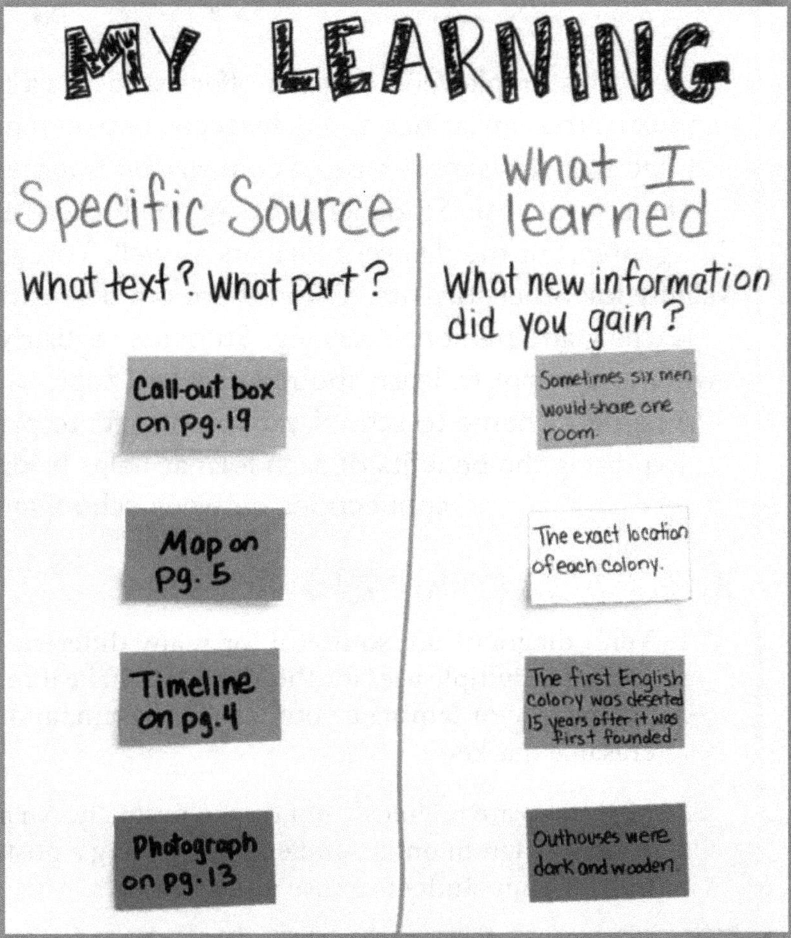

MY LEARNING

Specific Source What text? What part?	What I learned What new information did you gain?
Call-out box on pg.19	Sometimes six men would share one room.
Map on pg. 5	The exact location of each colony.
Timeline on pg.4	The first English colony was deserted 15 years after it was first founded.
Photograph on pg.13	Outhouses were dark and wooden.

Figure 7.4 *My Learning* chart

Print or Digital?

This simple Venn diagram offers students a familiar structure to compare the similarities and differences between print and digital text. I find that this simple type of comparison is a great starting point for the school year. Students not only need to understand the different genres, but the different formats as well. This also helps to provide validity for other formats. Often there is a delineation between school learning and personal learning. Students regularly use digital sources when they want to learn about a personal topic or an area of interest. When they come to school, the focus shifts to primarily printed text. Exploring the benefits of each format helps bridge the gap and build connections between school and personal learning.

Repurposing This Chart:

1. Venn diagrams are so useful for many different areas of study. You will find multiple uses for this chart. To make it reusable, simply leave off the title or laminate your Venn diagram, and write the title with erasable markers.

2. My circles are obviously not drawn perfectly. An alternative is to find a Venn diagram online and enlarge it using a poster maker. Laminate this for your students to use multiple times.

Interactive Digital Sources:

History Channel: Topics Feature (www.history.com/topics)
This website includes videos, articles, images, and interactive media features related to over one hundred topics. Students can easily compare these formats all from one location.

Biography Channel (www.biography.com)
This website includes biographical information about numerous people. There are also a wide variety of interactive elements here.

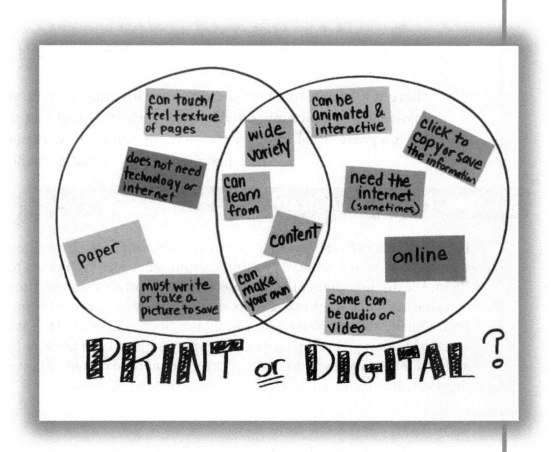

Figure 7.5 *Print or Digital?* chart

Reading is Not Just About the Words

There is a strong emphasis on evaluating literature, media, and informational text embedded in the standards. I find that this chart is a great visual to begin conversations about how readers use multiple formats to make meaning.

Creating This Chart:

I draw this chart from start to finish with students. I begin by writing the title and asking students to think about what reading means to them. We discuss their conceptions of reading, and spend some time just sharing what we think readers do when they look for information. During this conversation, I draw the book on the chart. I ask students to share what types of things they might find in a book or in a digital text. I add these ideas to sticky notes and post them all over the book. Just for fun, I add the eyes with the long eyelashes.

Variations:

- Color code your sticky notes based on the type of text it would most likely be found in.

- Add only one or two sticky notes when you first introduce the chart. Add additional sticky notes throughout the year as you introduce and go into more detail about the different structures.

- Use this as the activator for a scavenger hunt where students search for these features within different texts in your classroom.

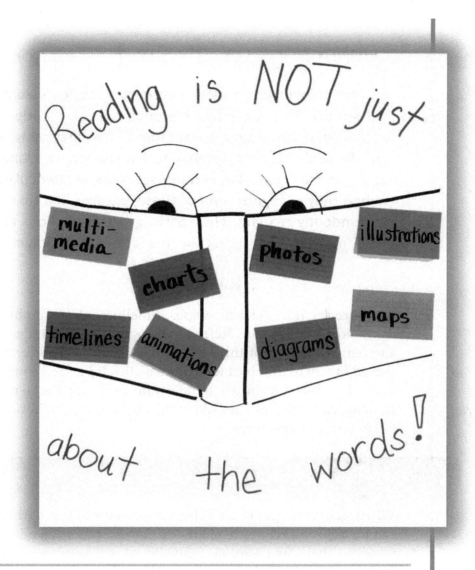

Figure 7.6 *Reading is Not Just About the Words* chart

Where Can I Find Information?

This colorful chart often becomes a staple in elementary classrooms. This is a great reference chart for students when they consider how a text is structured. This inevitably becomes one of those charts that you will notice students walking over to and using as they read. Elementary students, in particular, feel excited when they recognize one of these features in a text that they are independently reading. This sparks great discussions about why the author includes specific structures in a text.

Creating This Chart:

I prepare the titles (charts, graphs, timelines, photographs, paragraphs, animations) in advance. Refer to your grade-level standard to consider alternative versions of this list. I discuss these categories with students and add them to the chart with double-stick tape. We complete this chart over a few days. I really like to take time with each one to make sure that students can differentiate and see the obvious overlap between these different types of structures.

Writing Connection:

When students begin to craft short informational text of their own, this can be used as a reference chart. This offers students a bevy of features to use in their own writing. I usually ask students to use at least two of the features in their own pieces. This requires students to think like authors, and decide which features will best enhance their own communication. This is an effective starting point to help students analyze authors' choices.

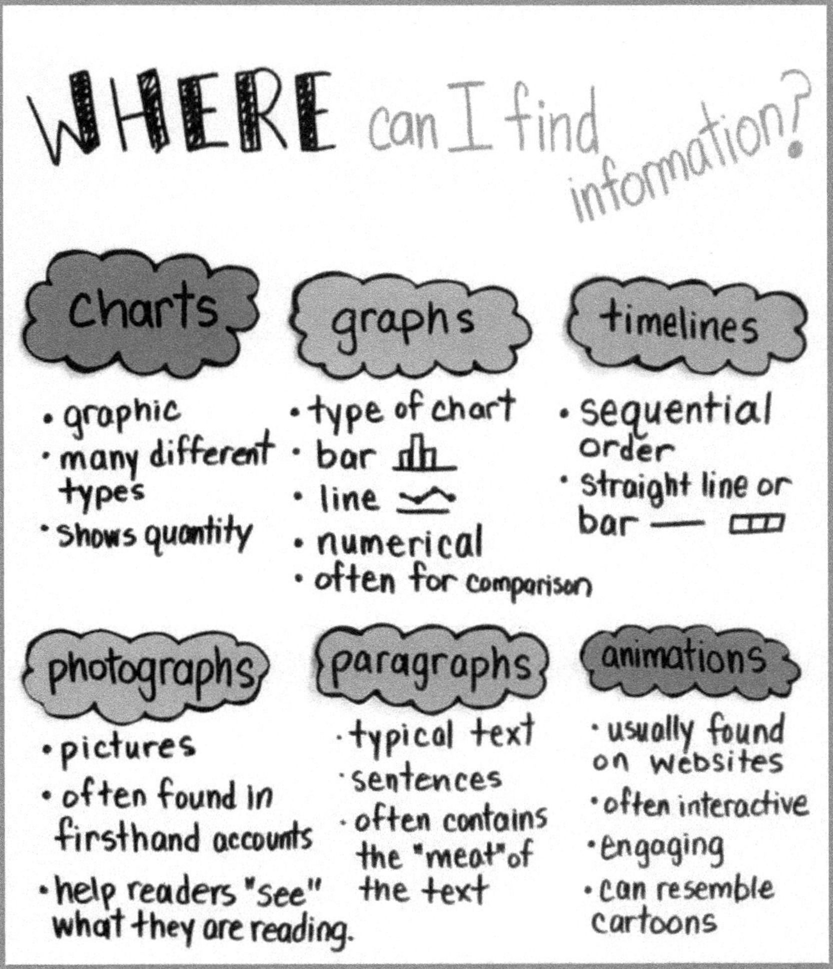

Figure 7.7 *Where Can I Find Information?* chart

Chapter 8

Evidence & Arguments

Common Core Reading Anchor Standard 8:
Delineate and evaluate the argument and specific claims in a text, including the validity of the reasoning as well as the relevance and sufficiency of the evidence.

	Literary Text	Informational Text
3rd	*(Not applicable to literature)*	*Describe the logical connection between particular sentences and paragraphs in a text (e.g., comparison, cause/effect, first/second/third in a sequence).*
4th	*(Not applicable to literature)*	*Explain how an author uses reasons and evidence to support particular points in a text.*
5th	*(Not applicable to literature)*	*Explain how an author uses reasons and evidence to support particular points in a text, identifying which reasons and evidence supports which point(s).*
6th	*(Not applicable to literature)*	*Trace and evaluate the argument and specific claims in a text, distinguishing claims that are supported by reasons and evidence from claims that are not.*
7th	*(Not applicable to literature)*	*Trace and evaluate the argument and specific claims in a text, assessing whether the reasoning is sound and the evidence is relevant and sufficient to support the claims.*
8th	*(Not applicable to literature)*	*Delineate and evaluate the argument and specific claims in a text, assessing whether the reasoning is sound and the evidence is relevant and sufficient; recognize when irrelevant evidence is introduced.*

Building Blocks of an Argument

When evaluating the strength of an argument, students are often told to examine the supporting details. The challenge with this directive is that many students are unclear about what supporting details really look like. This chart serves as a visual to help students see six specific details that an author might use to support an argument. This helps students to hone in and look for specific elements within a text.

Creating This Chart:

I write each word on red 8"x6" sticky notes to mimic the appearance of bricks. Explain to your students that these are just like the bricks of a house; they help to build a strong foundation for an argument. Students should be able to use this same concept when they discuss a text. *How strong is the argument? What types of support does the author have to develop his or her ideas?* Students can quantify what types of details they are reading and classify them using the blocks.

Variations:

- If you have a cinder block wall in your classroom consider skipping the chart paper altogether. Use the actual wall to create a wall anchor chart using the terms alone.

- Create a checklist for older students. List each of the six types and ask them to simply check off what the author uses in the text.

- Extend the checklist activity and ask students to not only look for different types of support, but to craft short paragraphs explaining that support.

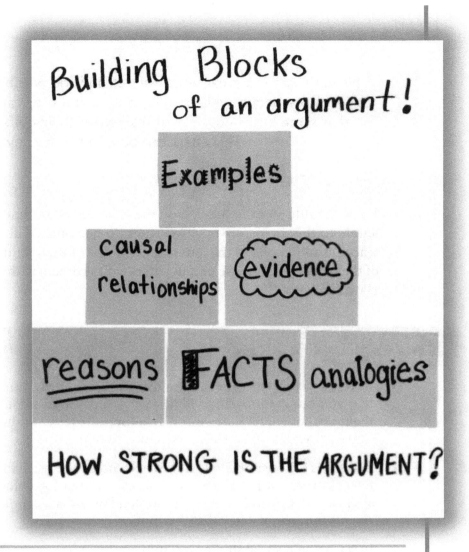

Figure 8.1 *Building Blocks of an Argument* chart

Evidence Suitcase

This fun chart is a great visual for reading and writing. Students can look for details while reading a text, and they can also apply that same knowledge when they write their own arguments. This chart can be adapted for any grade level.

Creating This Chart:

Draw the title and the suitcase on the chart ahead of time. Match the letters to the theme of your classroom to personalize it. I have seen teachers add jewels to the letters, put photos of their students on top of the letters, or even use precut letters to coordinate with their room. Have fun with it!

Teaching Ideas:

- Introduce each type of evidence using a news article or online text that you can read together. *Junior Scholastic* is a great (subscription required) source for current articles. There are also hundreds of free news articles and speeches at www.history.com.

- Make this a fun game! Pull off the sticky notes and place them in different corners of the room. Read an excerpt out loud slowly. Pause after each detail, and ask students to stand by the sticky note that represents the type of detail that they notice.

- In science and social studies, ask students to underline the supporting details, and then classify the *type* of detail.

- Create a color-coded suitcase! This can be done by writing the name of each type of evidence in a different color, or by using different color sticky notes for each type. When students read a text, ask them to underline the detail in the corresponding color.

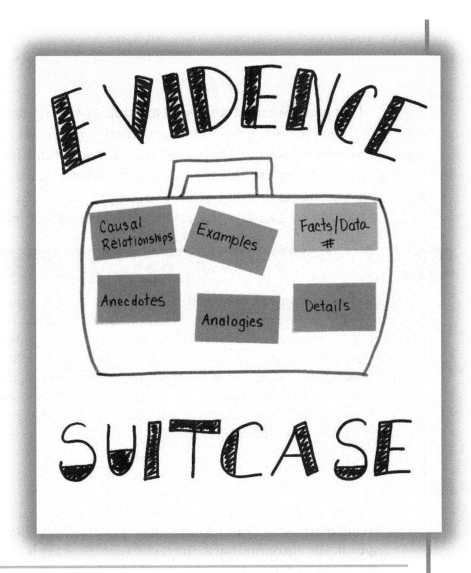

Figure 8.2 *Evidence Suitcase* chart

How Do Authors Support Their Claims?

This chart was created with a group of sixth graders. It works well for any grade, but particularly grades 5-12. Students in these grade levels will focus on claims much more intensively and frequently. Most of the other standards depend on the assumption that students in these grades recognize claims. Students will be expected to evaluate the validity and strength of multiple claims.

Creating This Chart:

I created this entire chart with students. For a more polished chart, draw your circles and the letters in advance or use bulletin board letters in matching fonts and colors to spell out *claim*. Spend time explaining what each example means. Show students a paragraph or text that cites evidence, makes an emotional appeal, includes examples, etc. You also want to discuss which strategies may overlap, which ones are stronger, and even spend time discussing which ways are most appropriate to support different types of claims.

Teaching Ideas:

- Some teachers like to introduce one or two letters at a time. You can go out of order and just focus on the types of support that students are specifically encountering in the text. Leave the other letters blank until you introduce them through authentic text examples.

- Challenge students to emulate the different types of support by writing their own examples. Consider assigning a writing prompt or argument and asking students to craft one or two different types of support for the argument. They don't need to write an essay or even a full paragraph. Students just need to show that they understand what that type of support might look like. Use fun topics that students will have a connection to.

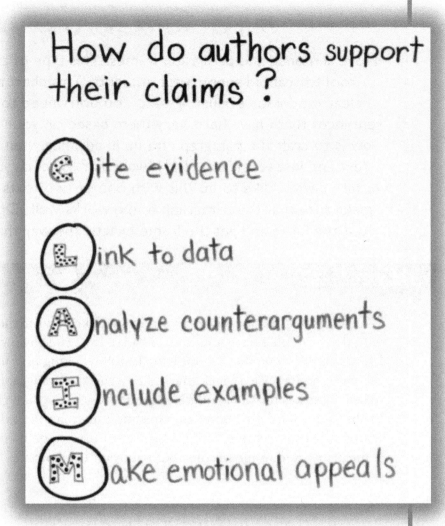

Figure 8.3 *How Do Authors Support Their Claims?* chart

Sound Reasoning or Not?

I love sentence and paragraph frames. This type of chart is a great tool to scaffold support for students. This chart also outlines a clear model for evaluating text. You don't need to use the same sentences that I have here, vary them based on your students. The key is to craft the paragraph frame in advance, then take an actual text and just test it out. *Did it work out? What do you need to add or take away?* I like to do this with one or two texts in advance to make sure that the paragraph frame works well. Do this to work out the kinks and get the frame exactly the way that you want it.

Creating This Chart:

When I create this chart with my students, I like to write the entire chart with them. While I have it written ahead of time (for my own guidance), I find that it is valuable for students to follow along and help me form the paragraph. I use a black marker to write the paragraph, but switch to a red marker for the blanks and parentheses. As you write, you want to think out loud and point out specific punctuation and transitional words that you may use. This is also a great time to deliberately include some clause and usage lessons that you want to reinforce.

Scaffolding & Differentiating:

After creating this chart with students, consider writing a paragraph together (using the frame) based on a shared text. Display this as a model for students. As students begin to master the paragraph frame, consider turning the words in the parentheses into a checklist. Finally, encourage students to share ideas and craft their own frames that serve the same purpose as the original chart here.

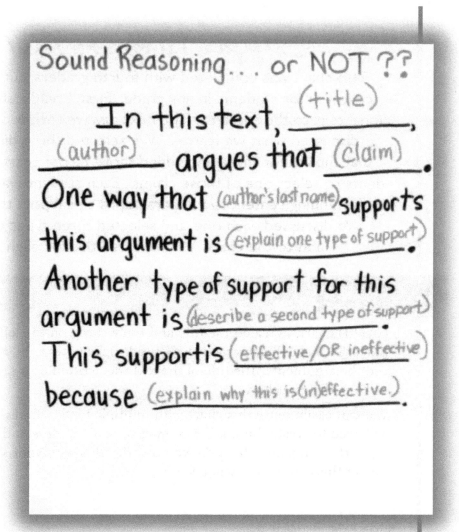

Figure 8.4 *Sound Reasoning or Not?* chart

Supporting Arguments!

This chart was completed with fourth graders, but can easily be replicated for students in any grade. First, I read a short informational text to the students. The next day, we revisited the text and discussed what we learned. We selected three different claims that the author made and added those to the chart. I asked students to select one of those claims. Each student was responsible for finding sentences and paragraphs to support that argument. We discussed each one, and selected three types of support to add to the chart. We repeated this for each of the claims.

Creating This Chart:

For this chart, I created the title and the writing on the left side in advance. To make this interactive, we used sticky notes to add the support and the arguments. The title of the text was written on a sentence strip and taped to the chart.

You can easily reuse this chart with multiple texts. I find that students will need to create this chart 3-5 times to really understand how details support arguments. The more you practice this with your students, the clearer this connection will become.

Teaching Ideas:

- Deliberately add details that do not support a claim and ask students to determine which ones don't belong or don't make sense.

- Mix up the sticky notes and ask students to sort out which are claims and which are details.

- Skip the chart altogether! Use the wall, the back of your classroom door, or even the floor to categorize the claims and supporting details.

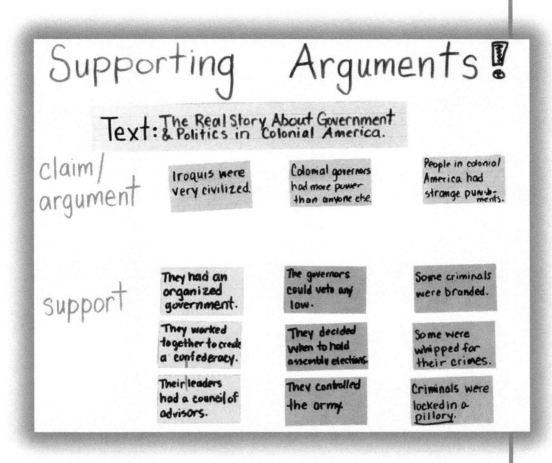

Supporting Arguments❗

Text: The Real Story About Government & Politics in Colonial America.

claim/argument	Iroquis were very civilized.	Colonial governors had more power than anyone else.	People in colonial America had strange punishments.
support	They had an organized government.	The governors could veto any law.	Some criminals were branded.
	They worked together to create a confederacy.	They decided when to hold assembly elections.	Some were whipped for their crimes.
	Their leaders had a council of advisors.	They controlled the army.	Criminals were locked in a pillory.

Figure 8.5 *Supporting Arguments!* chart

Chapter 9

Multiple Sources

Common Core Reading Anchor Standard 9:
Analyze how two or more texts address similar themes or topics in order to build knowledge or to compare the approaches the authors take.

	Literary Text	Informational Text
3rd	Compare and contrast the themes, settings, and plots of stories written by the same author about the same or similar characters (e.g., in books from a series).	Compare and contrast the most important points and key details presented in two texts on the same topic.
4th	Compare and contrast the treatment of similar themes and topics (e.g., opposition of good and evil) and patterns of events (e.g., the quest) in stories, myths, and traditional literature from different cultures.	Integrate information from two texts on the same topic in order to write or speak about the subject knowledgeably.
5th	Compare and contrast stories in the same genre (e.g., mysteries and adventure stories) on their approaches to similar themes and topics.	Integrate information from several texts on the same topic in order to write or speak about the subject knowledgeably.
6th	Compare and contrast texts in different forms or genres (e.g., stories and poems; historical novels and fantasy stories) in terms of their approaches to similar themes and topics.	Compare and contrast one author's presentation of events with that of another (e.g., a memoir written by and a biography on the same person).
7th	Compare and contrast a fictional portrayal of a time, place, or character and a historical account of the same period as a means or understanding how authors of fiction use or alter history.	Analyze how two or more authors writing about the same topic shape their presentations of key information by emphasizing the different evidence or advancing different interpretations of facts.
8th	Analyze how a modern work of fiction draws on themes, patterns of events, or character types from myths, traditional stories, or religious works such as the Bible, including describing how the material is rendered new.	Analyze a case in which two or more texts provide conflicting information on the same topic and identify where the texts disagree on matters of fact or interpretation.

Book Face-Off

This chart might just be my favorite chart to use with students. This is such an effective visual to help students compare two different books. The interactive nature of the chart also makes it reusable with multiple books.

Teaching With This Chart:

1. This chart is for comparing two different books. In this instance, we compared *The BFG* and *The Twits* as part of a larger Roald Dahl unit.

2. Draw your silhouettes and title in advance.

3. Write the story elements that you want to focus on in the middle of the two silhouettes.

4. Lead a discussion with students to identify the characteristics of each book. Then, write these on sticky notes and place them inside of the corresponding silhouette.

Variations:

- Create and laminate this chart with the title and silhouettes only. Use dry-erase markers and different color sticky notes to reuse this chart with different texts.

- Instead of making one chart, make two or three. Students can use these in groups to compare texts at the same time. You can still keep the original chart up in the classroom for students to reference.

- Color-code the sticky notes according to elements that are unique to each book and use a third color for qualities that are present in both.

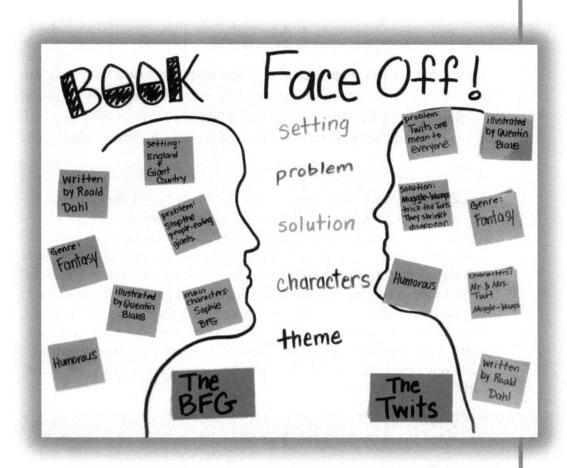

Figure 9.1 *Book Face-Off* chart

Comparing Texts

This chart works well with any grade level. This one was created with fifth graders using literature. We had just read Judy Blume's *Blubber* and Barthe DeClement's *Nothing's Fair in Fifth Grade*. I selected these books because of the similar story elements.

Creating This Chart:

Aside from the title, this entire chart was created with the students. Be sure to use sticky notes for each part of the chart (except for the headings) so that you can move things around and reuse the chart with different books. For the story element section you can vary your choices to tailor your instruction to your students. We used different color sticky notes to focus on setting, character, theme, and problem for our chart. You can use this chart to explore the conflict, resolution, setbacks, or any aspect that you want to target. This section does not need to remain static. After discussing the story elements in each book, ask students to point out similarities and differences. Record these on sticky notes and add them to the chart.

Teaching Ideas:

- Use this chart to compare books by the same author or in the same genre (fantasy, mystery, etc.).

- Create an organizer that mirrors this larger chart for students to complete individually.

- Introduce this standard by comparing fractured fairy tales (fairy tales written from an alternative point of view) to traditional fairy tales. A couple of my favorites are: *Honestly, Red Riding Hood Was Rotten!: The Story of Little Red Riding Hood as Told by the Wolf (The Other Side of the Story)* and *Seriously, Cinderella Is SO Annoying!: The Story of Cinderella as Told by the Wicked Stepmother (The Other Side of the Story)*, both written by Trisha Speed Shaskan.

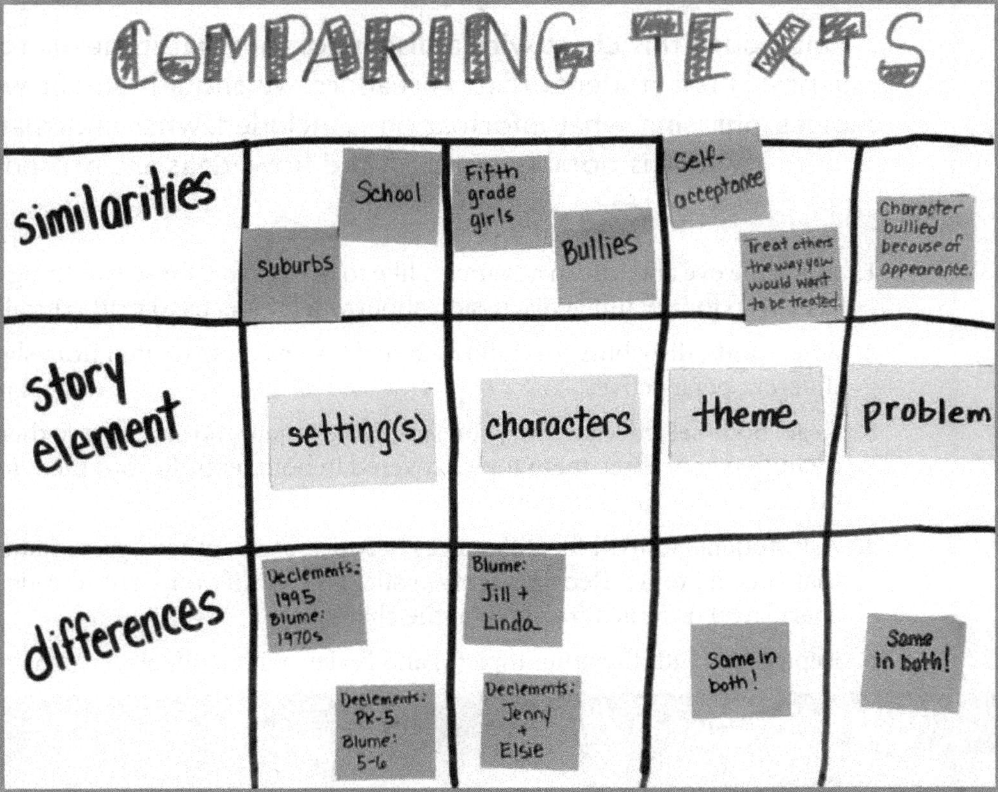

Figure 9.2 *Comparing Texts* chart

A Critical Eye

I introduce this chart with a discussion of what it means to be critical. I tell students that, as readers, we should look at word choices, phrasing, what information is included, what information is notably omitted, and how ideas are presented.

Creating This Chart:

1. Draw the eye and title in advance. I like to display just those two things as a backdrop for my initial discussion about what it means to read critically.

2. Afterwards, distribute two informational text excerpts written from slightly different perspectives.

3. Read both selections with your students. When you finish, ask them to identify two or three main topics covered in both texts. Record these topics on the left side of your chart.

4. Ask students to look for differences between each authors' presentation of that specific topic. Record these on sticky notes (if you want to reuse the chart later) or write directly onto the chart.

5. Repeat this with the other topic(s) and review with students.

Writing Connection:

Students can analyze their own writing for this standard. To do this, select one or more online news articles. Ask students to read the article, then write their own short articles on the same topic. Critically analyze those different articles, using this chart.

Informational Text Sources:

A quick and easy source for informational text is to craft your own! This also gives you the opportunity to deliberately create nuanced differences and vary the difficulty level. Alternatively, you can find great informational text sources online:

- **CNN Student News** (www.cnn.com/studentnews)
- **National Geographic News** (www.nationalgeographic.com/news)
- **The History Channel** (www.history.com/news)

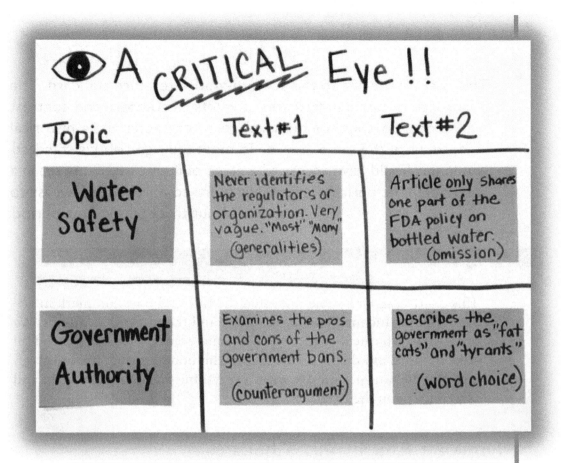

Figure 9.3 *A Critical Eye* chart

Fact or Fiction?

This chart is specific to the seventh-grade literature standard. The language of this standard asks students to compare and contrast a fictional portrayal of a time, place, or character and a historical account of the same period. To meet the rigor of this standard, students should have access to a piece of literature that is set in a notable time period. This allows more comprehensive access to material about that specific time period.

Creating This Chart:

This chart is also reusable. I created the title and question mark in advance. With students, I added the lines and the category headings. We discussed each category (people, time, and events) together. I called on students to share differences between the book and the historical account of the time period. We wrote everything on large sticky notes and placed them on the chart.

Thinking About Text Choices:

Try to select a text that students have already developed background knowledge about, involves characters close to their age, and can be read independently by most students. You want everyone to have access to the strategies here. As the year goes on, you will expose students to more complex and increasingly difficult text. This is not necessary, nor particularly useful, when first introducing a standard.

We read *The Witch of Blackbird Pond* by Elizabeth George Speare. This novel is set in a Puritan colony in the late 17th century. Our research covered the decade just before the events in the book. I decided that this was appropriate as long as the research covered Puritanism, the Quakers, and colonial Connecticut. You will want to establish your own guidelines.

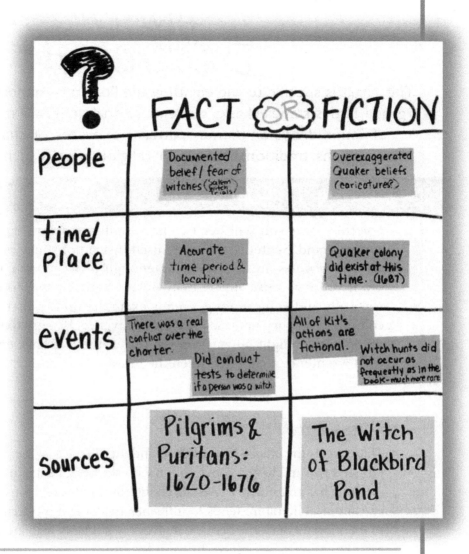

Figure 9.4 *Fact or Fiction?* chart

How Does the Old Influence the New?

This chart is specific to the eighth-grade literature standard. The language of this standard asks students to analyze how a modern work of fiction draws on themes, patterns of events, or character types from myths, traditional stories, or religious works such as *The Bible*.

Creating This Chart:

For this chart you will need to have sentence strips, tape, and scissors on hand. Sentence strips are used instead of sticky notes because the sticky notes are just not long enough to write your information on. If you try to use larger sticky notes, they take up too much room vertically and you cannot get many examples on the chart. Create the columns, category names, and title in advance. Be sure to space out or measure the height of your rows to make sure you have enough space to fit a sentence strip in between the lines.

Introducing This Chart:

This chart is the official kick-off for standard nine. I post the standard, then I just sit down and have a conversation with students. I explain that almost everything has an influence. We talk about how myths, religious texts, and older, canonical literature tends to influence media and modern writing. I like to mention media here, because it gives my students who are not avid readers a larger set of references to consider for this conversation. Next, I share an example of something that is modern that the students readily know and understand. Then, I explain what traditional influence that example draws from. I neatly write it on a sentence strip, cut off any excess, then, tape it on the chart. After one or two examples, most of your students will be clamoring to share their own examples. Some of their examples will be silly or have weak connections. Despite the silliness, I include all examples. As long as they can explain the connection or influence, I tape it to the chart.

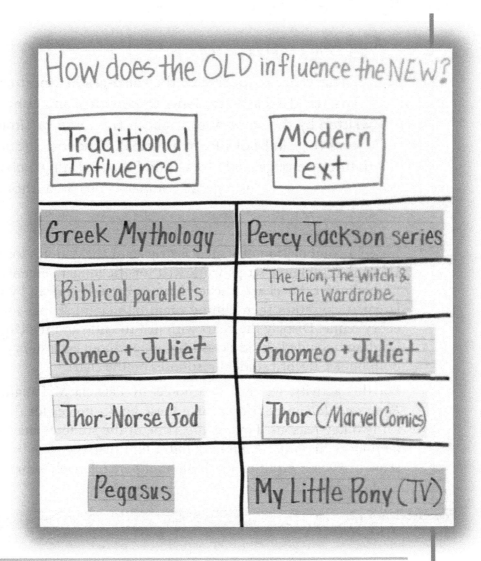

Figure 9.5 *How Does the Old Influence the New?* chart

Same Author. . . Different Text

This chart is specific to the third-grade literature standard. The standard asks students to compare and contrast stories written by the same author about the same or similar characters (e.g., in books from a series). Students should focus on themes, settings, and plots. I find that creating a chart like this is a great companion to an author study unit.

Creating This Chart:

I used a combination of sentence strips and sticky notes for this chart. I find that sentence strips work well for the longer sentences that are necessary for this chart. The left hand column is created by writing on larger sticky notes then cutting them into cloud shapes for each category name. Display the chart with just the title and the cloud-shaped headings included. Lead a class discussion about each story element for both books. Record student responses on the chart.

For this activity, we read two books by Patricia McLaughlin: *Sarah, Plain and Tall* and *Skylark*. I like these book choices for third graders for two key reasons. First, while some of the students may already be familiar with *Sarah, Plain and Tall*, I find that very few have read the sequel, *Skylark*. Additionally, both books are relatively short and can be read quickly.

Teaching Ideas:

- Roald Dahl books offer a wide variety of choices for different reading levels. Short books, like *The Twits* and *The Magic Finger* are high-interest, but easy to read. *Charlie and the Chocolate Factory* and *James and the Giant Peach,* on the other hand, are longer and require more reading stamina.

- Other great choices include books by Louis Sachar, Beverly Cleary, and Judy Blume.

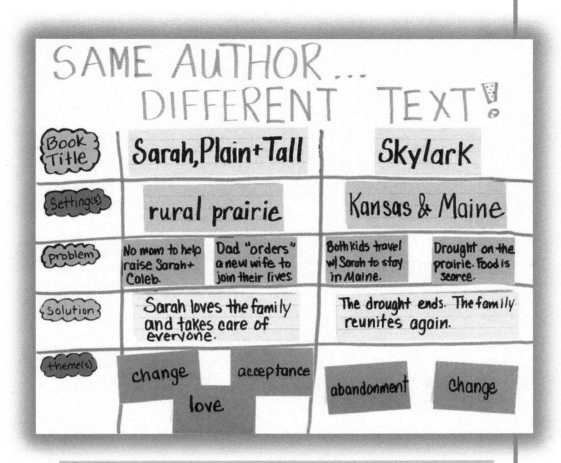

Figure 9.6 *Same Author . . . Different Text* chart

Notes

Notes

Final Thoughts . . .

Whether you are a novice or a veteran teacher, I hope that **Chart Sense**™ has ignited a passion for using visual aids in the classroom. Visual aids, when created with your students, are meaningful and resonate with readers. Being an artist or creating the most colorful and attractive chart is never the focus. The goal is to create mental images that help readers. Obviously, you will not need every chart in this book, but I hope that the charts you create with your readers are powerful. Creating charts with your students not only strengthens your reading instruction, but inspires a strong sense of shared learning in your classroom. Ready to continue the conversation? Join me online at **www.rozlinder.com** for even more teaching ideas or to ask questions and collaborate. Happy reading!

Dr. Roz